Inspire
Pilgr·image

Spain & Portugal

Camino Travel Tales and Tremendous Times

Garry McDougall

Revised and Updated
Second edition, 2017

Travelers of the world, wise, brave and foolish,
*this book of short story, poetry and photography
is dedicated to you.*

Pil·grim·age

1. A journey to a sacred place or shrine.
2. A long journey, usually one of exalted purpose or moral significance.

The word **pilgrimage** often conjures journeys into the land of miracles, angels, and saints, travels to sacred lands or fakery and self-serving legends.

If the journey-is-more-important-than the-destination, then long distance walking is a great vehicle for the human spirit. Regardless of spiritual affiliations, everyone has the right to pilgrimage.

Pilgrimage is reconceived as an act of the imagination. So *Inspire...* is written with wit, wisdom, humour and affection, for pilgrims and locals alike. Each town, story of poetica is sharply observed, especially in Tribute to Bermeo.

Its research uncover peculiar and surprising histories: the black Madonna cult, the privileged storks, the personality of architecture, odd tourism brochures and chickens cooped in cathedrals.

This series of short, lyrical poetica and tremendous, colourful tales have been long admired, as they explore small Spanish towns and Portuguese paths with a insightful, compassionate and sharp mind, observing and meeting travelers and locals along the way.

They are written for you, with persistent reworking of every word, striving for their full weight, resonance, intensity and color. So join the pilgrimage- its tales written by, and for, the curious and adventurous reader.

Delve into them. Feel free to add your thoughts, memories, stories and ideas at www.facebook.com/groups/535976469757492/ It could be the start of your beautiful journey.

Pilgrimage

Spain & Portugal

Many thanks to my fellow travelers,
Virginia, Anna and the authors of
the Write-On: Sarah, Stuart, Helena, Julia, Karen, Nore, Michelle and Cindy.

Firstpress Australia
Copyright 2017 ©
ISBN 9780648063605

Spain & Portugal • Inspire

Pilgrimage

Contents

What is Pilgrimage? Foreword and Map

SPAIN

1- Suite **St Jean Pied du Port,** Basque France PAGE 9
2- **St Jean Pied du Port,** Basque France PAGE 13
3- Chains of Enchantment, **Roncesvalles** Navarre PAGE 19
4- Beating Time, and Underdog, **Belorado** La Rioja PAGE 21
5- Indifference, **Los Arcos** La Rioja PAGE 25
6- From **Triacastela**, Galicia PAGE 32
7- To **St Domingo**, La Rioja PAGE 33
8- Lost in Translation, **St Domingo**, La Rioja PAGE 35
9- To The **Meset**a Castille and Leon PAGE 40
10- Astorga Suite, **Astorga** Leon PAGE 43
11- Pilgrim **Astorga** Leon PAGE 46
12 - Like a Bird Meseta Spain PAGE 52
13- **Marvelous Najera** La Rioja PAGE 53
14- These Birds Have Flown, **St Domingo de la Calzada** PAGE 58
15- **Cordillera Cantrabrica** Leon and Bierzo PAGE 61
16 - **Picos d'Europa** (Garganta) Cantabrica & Asturias PAGE 67
17- Tribute to **Arzua** La Rioja PAGE 71
18- Building, from **Palas de Rey** Galicia PAGE 75
19- Drive-by Hooting, **Santiago de Compostela** Galicia PAGE 76
20- **Farewell Santiago** Galicia PAGE 79
21- **Tribute to Bermeo** Basque Spain PAGE 80
22- **Segovia** Gallery (photos) PAGE 87

Pilgrimage

SPAIN

Compendium to *Damn!* (Leon to Santiago) PAGE 90
23- **Portomarin** Galicia PAGE 92
24- Let Me Die -Short Story **O'Cebriero** PAGE 94
25- In a Bowl Galicia PAGE 98
26 and 27- Proud Tortilla & Morrow Morn PAGE 99
28- Very, Very (Bad English) **Leon** PAGE 101
29- Fuego, en route to **Astorga** PAGE 103
30- Shadowland PAGE 105
31- By An Alberge Galicia PAGE 107
32- At The Counter, **Triacastela** Galicia PAGE 108
33- Weatherman Rules PAGE 109
34- My **Palas de Rey** Galicia PAGE 110

Camino P O R T U G A L

Porto

1- The Buccaneers Return PAGE 112
2- The Last Sardine, **Porto** PAGE 124
3- Morning Porto, Porto Belly PAGE 130

On The Road: Porto to Santiago

4.-Roads End, Porto PAGE 132
5- Stones Wait PAGE 135
6- The Cuban PAGE 137
7- Only for Poetry PAGE 138
8- Without Thinking PAGE 140
Further Information, web links, etc, PAGE 141

FOREWORD

Whether you have walked the Camino de Santiago, are considering it, or are simply drawn to the people, land and cultures of Spain and Portugal, *Pilgrimage's* stories and poetica offers pleasure, humour and inspiration.

Your journey starts inside France, from St Jean Pied du Port, the traditional starting point for the eight-hundred kilometre walk through northern Spain known as the Camino Frances.

You are on pilgrimage to Santiago de Compostela in Galicia, but what is more important: the journey or the destination?

His style is imaginative, colourful and direct, making his people and experiences compelling: from medieval ice carriers, eccentric country festivals to chickens cooped in a cathedral, ghosts from the past are always pressing. Each piece is written with an unflinching eye and an enquiring mind. His unusual 'take' on events catch us by surprise, taking us where we least expect.

In the hands of a poet, storyteller and novelist, it is often 'ordinary' life that impress us thr most. In the small towns and large like Los Arcos, Astorga and Pals de Rey, we experience small and eccentric events that take on unexpected significances. We unexpectedly enter an intense and lyrical world, always sympathetic to people's affections, vulnerabilities, needs and courage.

His delightful photographs are an additional link to his stories, sometimes ironic and comic. What surrounds people embodies Spain, Portugal and their peoples, just as they charm and envelope visitors.

Read, absorb and enjoy. You'll treasure it.

The Many Ways to Santiago de Compostela

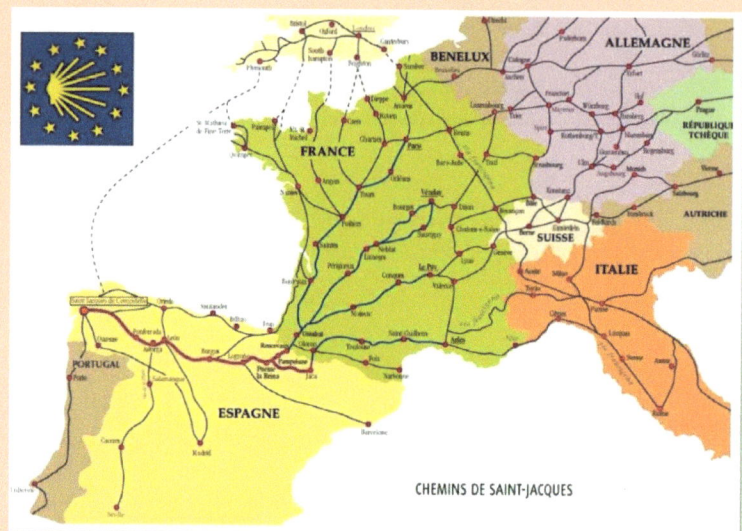

The **Camino Frances** from St Jean Pied de Port across Northern Spain. Other paths start in France, Spain & Portugal, all leading to Santiago de Compostela. (EU)

Some people from my first walking group, about to leave Roncesvalles.

1 Suite St Jean Pied de Port
Start at the France Border

'Pour qua Ostabat?' says the woman at the information desk. Having arrived at St Jean Pied de Port, where thousands of people start their pilgrimage to Santiago, she asks why are you starting *your* journey from Ostabat, twenty-eight kilometres before St Jean? Her rippling forehead persists: Why?

True, many pilgrims (or peligrinos) arrive here from Geneva, Amsterdam or Berlin., entering St Jean's northern gate after long treks from Le Puy, Vezeley, Tour or more cities. For them, St Jean might be their journey's end. For others, it is part of a longer, complete pilgrimage to Santiago de Compostela. But starting from Ostabat, only twenty kilometres before St Jean? Why?

'Un peu randonnee en France. Beaucoup kilometre en Espagne', I answer, in a desperate attempt to explain myself. Our group will be walking long distances through Spain in the coming weeks. By starting from Ostabat, we will enjoy a little more of lush, Basque France before reaching the drier Spanish landscape after Pamplona and Burgos

What I would love to have said, in French, is that Ostabat is a great starting point, as it is here that the three classical European pathways converge: the Via Podiensis from Le Puy-en-Valey, the Via Lemovicensis from Vezeley and Via Turenensis from Tours. On this high hill, ancient thousands of Swiss, Saxon, Scot, Russian, German Italian, French and Polish pilgrims met, people of different languages, traditions and cultures. Perhaps they had never known of each other. This hilltop was- and still is- the meeting place of wayfarers, gifted each other's company, and glorious Pyrenees views, a suitable starting for my adventurous group.

Our journey began next morning on a narrow farm road outside **St Palais**. Stretching our legs for the first time, we climbed a rutted, earthen road to high **Ostabat**. On an auspicious, fine day, the world stretched before us, we pelegrinos-to-be, keen to rise to the occasion, rise to the challenge, rise to peaks, and rise early, eager for the day ahead.

On Ostabat's grassy hilltop we met a white, three-sided enclosure, half-chapel, half-picnic area, with panoramic views. A curious plaque read:

> Erautitsi Gai chtoet arik
> Begira Gait zatzu Yauna
> othoitz Egizu Guretzat
> ama Birjina. 1894

Not French, English, German or Spanish; it is Basque, the local language- spoken, fought and encountered as the second, third or maybe tenth language met by ancient and modern pilgrims.

Sitting down to cheese, *chorizo*, bread and fruit, we opened the map. The Camino was poorly signposted from here, although the *pelegrino's* (or pilgrim) habit of marking the route with stone cairns provides us some useful signage for the days ahead. For a thousand years, pilgrims brought stones and other mementos from home, or along the way, at certain points leaving behind a token of their commitment to their sacred journey.

The map put away, on the nearby rise we saw a single ram, a statuesque sentry standing high atop a rusting shed. What!? The surrounding herd stared in adoration and bewilderment. It seemed Basques breed leaders even amongst sheep.

Equally compelling was the distant mountains - Etxehortia at 1704m, Pic d' Oihi at 2017m, Pic d' Midi, 2872m, jagged peaks marking the Pyrenees' backbone, growing ever lofty and muscular towards the Mediterranean, the peaks diminishing towards the Sea of Biscay, **Bayonne** and **San Sebastian**.

Large red-roofed houses dotted the Basque valleys, lush green pastures fringed with forest, sweeping, tempestuous rain squalls beyond, performing like acrobats against their mountainous backdrop, swift grey and white clouds with rain veils beneath, softened the landscape. Here and there were patches of blue, the scene as richly coloured as opal.

Wham- a burst of wind and pelting rain hit us. We retreated from the marauding storm clouds to our protective shelter. Stray from here, and even our wet-weather gear would fail us.

'Keep your wits about you', I warned. Many pilgrims had perished through carelessness or poor preparation.

Eventually the shower passed, and I was struck with the scale of our undertaking, an 830 km journey to Santiago de Compostela. What a challenge coping with the extremes of weather, the outdoor's obstacles, the self-reliance required, and encountering numerous physical concerns.

Taking the forest track downhill, we soon entered that intimate world of lush green forest, slippery mud, persisting grasses, knotted tree roots, twigs and rotting leaves, the air dank, the pent up stillness only broken by a fleeing bird.

Arriving at a clearing, farmhouse and barn, we see pastures surrounded by narrow valley wood, and more, muddy track. Passing the local farmhouse like trespassers, no one seen, a curious dog stood by the fencing, a trailer-like container of ten thousand carrots, open to the birds. We reckon it was food for livestock, perhaps making wondrous carroty milk or orange pork.

Just beyond, was a ruinous structure, strangely facing up-valley, away from our searching eyes, its interior seen through a keyhole as big as your fist- a wooden altarpiece, paintings and icons as ancient as the hills. Above the door were a Maltese cross and a five-pointed star. This is **Harambeltz** with its chapel of Saint-Nicolas (patron saint of travelers) of twelfth, thirteenth and seventeenth century origins. Here was the last remains of a priory hospital for pilgrims, upheld by a Basque tradition of *donats*. We are told that, four local families, generation after generation cared for it. It was a shrine not a church, the building locked away from all but our searching eyes, its interior seen through a keyhole as big as your fist- a wooden altarpiece, paintings and icons as ancient as the hills.

Above the door were a Maltese cross and a five-pointed star. Harambeltz I realized, the chapel of Saint-Nicolas, patron saint of travellers, for twelfth, thirteenth and seventeenth century pilgrims. Here are last remains of a priory hospital for pilgrims, upheld by a Basque tradition of donats. We are told that four local families, generation after generation, carry the keys, the last lay communities dedicated to the priory and hospital, bound by vows of minor obedience, poverty and chastity in widowhood. The donats worked for the priory order at the service of pilgrims- a gem so easily passed, our curiosity rewarded.

Other pilgrims passed without noticing. We are not alone. In many places we will be drawn to and pass by abundant religious art and local architecture. Amongst the journey's many pleasures and

challenges, will be traversing Nature's thickets and muddy tracks, striding alongside minor highways, seeing the vast open plains of the *meseta* and its expansive countryside, climbing and descending the steep sierras.

So many excited people today. When the journey from **Ostabat** started so well, you think 'this can't be so difficult.' One day at a time, always the best with long distance walking. It took heart not strength, patience, not religion or bicycles. Most of all; it was about heart and organisation.

In the days ahead we'd meet plenty of people with heart; conversing with them in the languages of words, faces, hand gestures and food, staying in tents, communal hostels, small hotels, *alberges* or *pensions*, letting our curiosity occasionally lead us to great wonders, every day, revealing our strengths and weaknesses, like Tinman, Lion and Scarecrow in the Wizard of Oz, confronting the quirks, quibbles, anxieties and worries that dog us. You wonder: when life's demands retreat, and all our basic needs are satisfied, perhaps the journey will reveal our social, helpful and sharing natures, and many friendships made along the way.

After a snack at **Larceveau**, the sun reappears. I grab my being, put bread and cheese between my teeth, and we set off for St Jean Pied de Port. To the start.

2 *Journey to* **St Jean Pied de Port**

A few years later, my wife and I reached **St Jean** via charming, gritty and grounded **Bayonne**, taking the slow and pleasant single-carriage train with two staff and a dozen passengers. Meandering across the plain, intersecting, over passing and under-reaching its waters, the low hills around us built as we approached the Pyrenees. The vegetation thickened where our track paralleled the River Nive with lush greenery around **Cambo-les-Bains**. Thereafter the river's course denies roadway, our rail line winding through narrow woods like a curious and affectionate cat slinking through steep and isolated forest and vale.

Remote halt. Our train stoppped for no apparent reason. Delayed for minutes longer, silence begged the question: what was happening? Patience is a virtue for some, but we curious passengers put our heads out the window or leaned from the doors for a better view. The driver's assistant had jumped from the train, his time spent shooing sheep off the line.

Shoo! No luck with one of them. It took a few steps down the line, and seeing the steep bank to one side, blackberries and fencing on the other, the woolly one was staying on track for as long as possible. Shoo. Its dainty feet trod the treacherous sleepers- Shoo. It was one anxious animal.

Hoot. Hoot. The train driver had his way, the assistant still 'shooing' until the woolie-jumper found greener pastures. Late arrival in St Jean- we're laughing.

St Jean Pied de Port

Thinking of you St Jean
Pied de Port,
Basque town in the Pyrenees foothills
registering pilgrims, issuing *credentiales*
and overnight dreams,
hospitale accommodation and
alberges along the Way;
pilgrim advice and information
for your Pyrenees crossing

to Roncesvalles and Burguette
occasioning death and distress before now
three-decade volunteers sometimes fearful
urging preparedness, when bound to snow.

Everyday arrivals from Le Puy-en-Valey
Vezelay, Tours and beyond
all north, east and western Europe
coming to you with pebbles in their pockets
and fire in their bellies.

St Jean, Basque town of two thousand
the dreamers drifting your cobblestone street
the old town's dipping, curving medieval path
past sturdy stone houses
albergues and Camino office,

meeting the lower church
under arch, river and tower clock
listen to the wind
lean over your word stream,
hear anticipation's footsteps

be the here-and-now
Basque walls hold secrets
centuries as Navarrone
severity and piety as prison
embrace the Pyrenees hills
in sorrow and joy.

Visit St Jean- first time reconnaissance
exotic and strange
this pilgrimage town proclaiming itself
gateway Camino Frances
the Way to Santiago.
We come to you innocent
gifted great fondness
recalling a pilgrim's story
our innocence becomes us.

Tribute to St Jean

Roughly translated, St Jean Pied du Port is the 'foot-of-the-pass' a rare appellation defined by the tens of thousands of pilgrims putting one foot beyond the other- going that little bit further, seeing, hearing, sensing, moving towards Santiago, first steps over the Pyrenees.

We came to you, St Jean, not knowing your town or your Basque name of **Donibane Garazi**; not knowing another two-hundred-and-fifty-four 'St Jeans' in all France; this one with a quiet bar under azure sky, a cinema, supermarket, tall hills and Basque houses dotting the lower reaches, railway at your fringe.

A few kilometres away was another 'you'- **Saint-Jean-le-Vieux**, first pilgrim St Jean for centuries, razed to the ground in 1177 by Richard the Lionheart's troops, quelling the rebellious; the reborn downstream-St-Jean, built by Navarre, named after unfashionable Saint Jean, a peacemaker when warrior saints- St George, St Michael and Santiago the Moor Slayer- were pillagers, conquerors, virile crusaders and miracle workers against Moors, Jews and unbelievers.

In the C14th, Sancho the Strong added Notre-Dame-du-Bout-du-Pont, your red-schist Gothic church with bell tower, over Porte d'Espagne, commemorating 12 Battle of Las Navas de Tolosa, Moorish power undermined, new St Jean now rivaled Somport Pass and **Jaca** as favoured pass to southern Navarre, your tiny walled cite welcoming pilgrims from all Europe, drawing them away from Jaca, your sloping *Rue de la Citadelle* running down to river, bridge and church, facing yonder Pyrenees.

You hugged your hillside, cosied around warm hearths, your village no more than a few lanes within your modest but stern defenses against English, Norman and French bandits, everyone beating on your gates, royal Navarre reduced by Castile and Leon's onslaught. Later, alone and vulnerable, only pilgrims favoured you.

Avignon's popes built cold residence amongst you- a 'gaol'? purpose unknown, its C18th use (said to be) 'Prison des Eveques', its presence a sign of order as much as repression. The pilgrims came, your merchants of agriculture and cloth drew strength from mountain streams and forest grasses, St Jean Pied-du-Port little capital of upper Navarre. Your people's precious words, deeds and histories are written upon you, histories that sleep as vellum wiped clean, to be inscribed again with tomorrow successes. In the long and overlapping life of peoples, nothing is sacred. Long-built pilgrim traditions and associations, recede, reappear and disappear, are rediscovered, remade and recast for other's purposes. Many stories here. But nothing sacred.

You are become French, St Jean.

In 1620, by tortured bloodlines, royal deals, nasty intrigue and cruel betrayal, you became part of France, King Henry's private domains of Navarre and Bearn fortified by industrious Vauban, citadel fortification against the Spanish, a monolithic fortification over old St Jean, last defense against invaders, armies soldiers, protestants or rebels.

By then you were made of sterner stuff, gaol and citadel, sandstone walls, and gray-pink schist homes and shops, only softened by proud owner's names inscribed above your doors, one announcing 1789's price of bread. Too late- they traded bread for revolution, shaking, unmaking and replacing Royal rule, St Jean soon reformed, domesticated, and expanding beyond its unwanted walls. Only a few more revolutions between then and today.

What am I doing here?

On an internet post, one pilgrim-to-be wrote: '...at the foot of the French Pyrenees, I knew nothing of the journey upon which I set out. I found out this is a Catholic pilgrimage to honor St. James the Apostle. I discover that I need to wear a scallop shell, which reflects the Camino's pagan roots of fertility. I receive a pilgrim passport that needs a stamp from every church along the way. We will follow the Milky Way to *Finnistere*, known in medieval times as the end of the earth.'

Many others have been thinking, breathing, imagining this Camino to Santiago, an eight hundred kilometre journey annually drawing so many people from so many countries, passing under your Porte de *Espagne*, people from many professions, maybe financiers, sailors, filmmakers, families, grandparents, prisoners, salespeople and engineers, departing for Spain, Navarre and the Rioja.

Busy pilgrims-to-be are all geared up, prepared and ready, wondering what madness overtook them, what tests lie ahead. What's the purpose of journeying the Camino de Santiago? What pay or pain is ahead, over the Pyrenees and through forbidding Spain?

Departing St Jean Pied de Port, pilgrim's carry their anxiety with them, little or no time spent exploring the beautiful up river parkland to the old mill, the diversion track uphill to the citadel with its labyrinth defenses, the Saturdays markets outside the old wall, charming regional crafts that burden a backpack, Basque choral evenings, vineyards, cheeses and local cinema. What a rush!

Please, stay in St Jean one more night. Spend a little time seeing the afternoon pilgrims arriving at St Jean's northern gate, those adventurous ones coming from St Puy-en-Valey, Vezelay, Tours and beyond. Some have departed from the home doors in Brussels, Frankfurt or Lille, as they did for hundreds of years. Have a chat to them. Stand beneath the north Porte and its inscriptions. See the new arrivals, arms thrown out, smiles on their faces, or sometimes seen as plainly perplexed, exhausted and bewildered.

Now you know why they want to go. Looking to the rising hills, mind and senses awakened, conversations expanded and companion eyes widened. Red roofs, green hills, grey and white peaks - they are dreaming the colour of travel. St. Jack- we leave in the morning.

Early morning St John, outside the city walls.

View of St jean from the old walled town.

3 *Chains of Enchantment*

Roncesvalles, Navarre, Spain. When pilgrims cross the Pyrenees, their first stop is usually Roncesvalles, with its ancient abbey, featuring 'Charlemagne's Granary' and a few accommodation places. Down track is **Burguette**, an attractive village featured in Hemingway's *The Sun Also Rises.*

Three of us in a Spanish bar: me, the broken-hearted Italian and sensuous Susan- celebrating our snow-capped Pyrenees crossing, *vino tinto* in hand.

'Stay with me tonight Susan,' says the broken-hearted Italian.

He does not desire the grappa nor the somnambulant Cola-Cao (Spanish hot chocolate). It's one man's nightcap to hope, two men bewitched by beauty and passion, and three of us in sweet Hell.

Susan talks about her travels in Bolivia. Eyes distant, she'd rather recall her friend Wayne's fascination for liquor and dynamite, him three times a hospital patient in that explosive land. On his third visit, the nurse's mouth agape, her eyes asking Susan, asking Wayne, 'Aren't you–?', 'Isn't it you–?' 'No, no,' they say in unison, 'First time.'

Cuddly toys and Santa Claus put Wayne in hospital, the two of them unwanted reminders of his family's shambolic Chicago Christmases. Wayne wanted to destroy Santa and cuddly toys; and for that, he needed dynamite.

Boom! 'Glory be!' says Wayne. Ka- boom!

'Ouch! Shit. Blood.'

Susan said Wayne was 'so funny', even when he retreated to his hotel room with another woman. 'So-o-o funny.'

Enchanting Susan, hazel eyes, clear-skin, square face, dark, wavy hair, all enthusiasm, sensuality and intensity; Swiss, teaches street-children in Geneva; knows a few games, leans on time. 'Wayne was in his fifties,' she said. Rich. 'Has his own company. Never grew up. A mad man. Always drunk.' I raise an eyebrow to Wayne's world, holding her gaze. 'One night,' she said, catching her breathe, 'one night, we drank with an Irishman. And drink! And drink! I was floored.'

And next morning, still drunk, Wayne knocked on her door.

'Come in', said fearless Susan.

'I need a shower,' he said, not saying why he's couldn't have one in his own room.

Later, there's a crash. 'Oh shit. Far-kin hell.'

'Wayne? Are you all right?' There was low, implausible moaning. 'Are you naked? Are you dressed?'

'Yeh.'

'I come in and help.'

What do you expect: some Wayne-like maneuver, some pathetic, drunken appeal to sympathy and desire? No? Wayne has blood streaming down his face and arms. He's a mess. Slipped in the shower. Grabbed the curtain, collapsed the railing and the cistern, and everything crashed. The falling cistern broke the toilet, the free-flowing water, spreading all over the room. What a mess. Broken bath, shower, shattered toilet and water everywhere, mixed with blood, and somehow, enchanting Susan applied bandages.

The broke-hearted Italian and I have listened intently, not asking about Wayne's other hospital visits, or Susan's first-aid skills, hotel room design or Bolivian Christmases.

We sit up straight, eyes drooped, absorbing Susan's ardor.

Noticing a silent tradesman huddled around the bar, a blinking internet machine that will not accept mere money, and an ATM with a weak pulse, the spell is broken. Susan's eyes are elsewhere, and I realize that our fellow pilgrims have taken to their beds, reminded that it's March now, and *marche* tomorrow.

'Stay with me tonight Susan', says the amorous Italian.

Spying untimely Santa and his reindeers above the bar, pulling his leaden sleigh, me and the broken-hearted-Italian suffer the reins and chains of enchantment.

4   *Beating Time*

Belorado is a small town of two thousand or more inhabitants, located just outside of the western Rioja, and on the fringe of Basque country. Burgos is some distance to the west so the town, belonging nowhere, makes an identity of its own.

Its soils are patchy, the town's leather industry in long decline. The old part of town is probably larger than the 'new', with two churches, one for winter, one for summer. Caves have been scratched into the cliffs, and pilgrims and locals enjoy lively set of bars in its narrow lanes. Pilgrims usually arrive here from St Domingo de Calzada, stay overnight in its alberges and B&B-style accommodation before another two days walk to Burgos. If they're lucky, they'll arrive in time for the town's week-long Festival of the Onion.

The final night's demolition of 'the onion'. After it's been paraded around Belorado's narrow streets, the young making an immense amount of noise with drums and trumpets and bugles.

Beating Time

On the Rioja's dry plain, Belorado forever inhales the hot breath of summer, and exhales the sombre, grey mists of sinking autumn; in the splish-splash of a Spanish winter, reflecting on its dark millennia when once its duke challenged the mighty House of Burgos. The duke lost, and for centuries after, the village was stripped of its fine clothing. Without protective walls and grand castle, its enemies seemed everywhere. It knew no spring.

The village still coughs and splutters in irregular health, rubbing its wrinkled skin in leather and onions. Both churches have crumbling walls, the town's narrow streets clinging to tattered charm, begging for new life, but hears only rumbling trucks, tastes only diesel fumes.

For consolation, it has an annual festival of burning meat, beating drums, insistent trumpets and ritual sacrifice of the onion. The village heart beats faster. Wild men and women pump through the

The old highway through Belorado. Morning. 'Piel' mean leather.

narrow streets by night, beating, blowing, blasting their instruments, pounding the crumbling walls with raucous tunes. What's television? The irrepressible rhythms insist- Ghosts out! Ghosts. Ghost! Ring the bells. Bells! Bells! Ring the bells. Without peace, riotous exclamation must suffice. We all fear silence. *Silencio*. And the wounded Duke is heard, saying 'Do not bow to the silence. Never.

In the town square next morning, the week-long festival over, council's men and women sweep away cigarette butts, coke cans, wine bottles, cardboard, cracker wrappings and cast-off clothing; the streets in mighty disarray, anathema to the Western mind.

As mid-day approaches, youngsters abandon their brief slumbers to inhabit the streets again, though spent, bare-buttocked and bewildered. Hours earlier they had blasted out a mighty tune, waking men and mice, mothers and masons. What a racket! You awake; sit erect in your bed, clasping the clock. It's 4 am. Everyone hears the call: 'Hear ye! Hear ye. For we announce to you... the day's festivities are over. Ghosts are vanquished. Time to sleep.'

This Belorado is a hard place: hard pillows, hard earth, sharp corners, surrounded by treeless farmland, decorations at a minimum. Crops fail. Tools turn against you. The smart one betrays you. Some will block your path. History has a bitter heart in Spain. Stirred by the agony winds, ghostly semblances still roam the village by night, dusty kings, dictators, bishops and republicans wrestling in its laneways and apartment blocks.

The stranger best linger in a bar, bent before the *vino tinto* shrine, settling into a darkened corner, watching life & football, nursing *bocadillos* & sharing exclamations. Thirty clocks surround you, collected over fifty years, all beating time.

The owner grunts. Let the stray dogs and big ideas fight over the bones behind the *Calle Mayor*. Let the three-legged mongrels, thin, weak and weary, gaze into today's windows with uncomprehending eyes before merging into *diablo* walls.

You, Belorado; never subdued Belorado. Fond Belorado. History extracts its price.

---

* *Beating Time*, 'Highly Commended', Peter Cowan Short Story Competition

Underdog

Oh what a feeling, underdog-
racked, paled, patched, against-a-wall, animal,
demented, earthbound, woeful, eyes without wonder,
no bark or bite given or taken,
four thin legs say- bitch of a world.

Salt of the Earth, brick, sublime you
two-headed traveler in dust,
my camera ready makes today yesterday
in puzzling Spanish town,
Guernica over the hill.

Paw thing.
Dogged. Dog-eared. Dog-tired.
Where is your manger, my manger,
our bones of sustenance, our friends,
afternoon darkness encroaching?

Beware those who muddy the waters,
their buckets of money telling you
your pain is good, that they will suffer
on the golf courses of life,
on outcomes and incomes.

Underdogs- fight for better days,
benefit the whole-in-one
emerge from *diablo* walls,
tear time's texture as Lest we forget,
together demented, earthbound, dissolved.

5 *Indifference*

Los Arcos, Rioja region, Navarre, Spain

In the province and the autonomous community of Navarre, **Los Arcos** is a village of 1800 people, some 3000, counting its small vineyards and farms in its hills and dry plains. Its main produce is red peppers, asparagus, artichokes, grapes and wine.
Pilgrims of the Camino de Santiago reach Los Arcos after walking 21km from Estella, an easy day walk, some continuing to tiny Torros del Rio or Viana. Those staying overnight in Los Arcos depart next day for a 28km. walk to Logrono, effectively the Rioja's capital.

Outside the cite walls, 'New' Los Arcos. From my Hotel window.

With affection for the people of Los Arcos

Indifference

Los Arcos, scarred by
history's murderous and indecoraous ways
material kindnesses, a desert deception
periodic terrors, the certain work of mischievous spirits,
your city walls a people's prison
falls into domestic ruin, elbow-to-elbow adobe

cracked and crumbling in annual suns
eerie streets, scratch-menu bars
locals watch glorious football
handsome passion in cold eyes
faded photos pinned to shadows
more accusation than display.

You do not love, Los Arcos.
In the nineteen-fifties and sixties
you almost expired, drought
abandonment and backwardness
your unwanted fate
conformity and oppression
too much to bear.

When the Beatles sang *She Loves You*
(yeh, yeh, yeh)
the Stones, *Black is Black*
Elvis, his *Jailhouse Rock*
your last girls understood too much
hiding in cupboards, ears to the radio
pining for ice cream, boyfriends and more to love.

In your labyrinth lanes, a boy might
challenge himself, walking the Calle Major
by night, his own devil
looking down endless *Rua La Sema*

one-fuel town exploding before his eyes-
Superman to the rescue, while
two people in a dimly lit bar
grope each other, overwhelmed by the moon.

Scampering down *Calle Ramon*, streets without lighting
your boy frightens and thrills his devil self
glowing light at his feet, thinking its God's light
shiny stones receiving the moon
his mystery is a baker and merchandise
ragged shops and broken homes
run-down parent warning of evil spirits
ghost houses stare from ochre cliffs
where transfixed saints and hermits once dwelled
facing the open plain, where the world ends.

A girl was held back by more bad luck
no woman, or woman-to-be, leaving the sink of life
the laundry of time, the patchwork of place
but working the fields with the father
son and the Holy Ghost.
The priest had eyes for her
and a thousand years in Hell
telling her God's sun shines on Santa Maria's dark altar.
her sensing many days without wonder
only church's songbook notes as big as her heart
promised sonata and Sinatra, never arriving
late reconciled to the *Dark Side of the Moon*.

Her mother's recipes unchanged
she joined free Spain
forty year avalanche of music, ideas
pizza and pictures, ice creams for everyone
magazines free from priests on endless picnics
boring abbeys and uniformed, thin-eyed men
a trickle of unkempt pilgrims enter your ruins
seeing right past your steel to sparkling eyes.
Their hands clenched poles, not guns
jot notes in diaries as tiny as a pebble.

Los Arcos. Some describe you as 'sleepy'
but you are awake to nightmares
your Roman self destroyed, buried and lost
town reborn as enforced stage of the pilgrimage
Riojan town of Jewish moneychangers
farmers and traders of Navarre
in Castillian outlands, centuries of disruption-
pogroms, wars and extravagances
today's children splash in your shining pool
ever cautious of friendships and jolly pilgrims
Basque hills to the north.

Start again, Los Arcos as
pilgrim on a long day's walk-
approach your ruined self, see
Hermitage de San Sebastian to the right.
Go ahead, sip from your fountain waters
eye your curious hills, turn into *Calle Major*
and know your ruinous self-
yours bars hidden to the south
where pilgrims do not wander
no ready shops exciting.
Visitors ask of your indifference,
not knowing your suffering and resentments.

Ancient Los Arcos
penned-in on Sancho the Sixth's orders
your Church of Santa Maria
Twelfth century Romanesque
sprinklings of the Protogothic
bolster of Renaissance and Baroque-
artifice to suffering.

From your umbrella square
bright day pierces the unpromising,
Navarre's most spectacular organ
music to your ears, thunderous voice of rebuke
your attached cloister, silent authority, yet loud.

Keen-eyed women welcome us
command respect, invites curiosity

and donations, presents
the craftsmen's work, cracked, crumbling
and faded, pledging themselves to restoration-
indifference breached.

They care for your Solomon songbooks
gold sculptured altarpiece, upstairs stage
of sculpture and faded paintings,

centuries of religious ornamentation
source of your oppression
wealth acquired without honest tilling of the soil
gold acquired with the blood of a million dead Indians
stolen from Incas and others
wasted on Spanish armies, armaments
artifice and gentry
now yours to draw the world of pilgrims-
let a little prosperity lessen your weeping.

Pilgrims donate a few Euros for bright tomorrow
for Los Arcos, their eyes puzzling a glass coffin
life-size Christ with gory marks of torture
charity foreswearing muscular saints and
warriors with angel's wings
beheading enemies with the swords of wrath.

Los Arcos, your church is
pre-enlightenment drama for song and ritual
miracle oratory hovering in stale air
music from the heavens when
Spanish empire peaked
wealth transacted in overblown sculptures
decoration and hollow words
in wood, gold and silver.

Hefty illusion, Spanish glory
sirens, centaurs, monsters, newts
and the great nothing, like TV repeats
everyone knows the story, towing-the-line
chanting the mantra, the dogma
happy ending never delivered

not in this world;
centuries of disappointments
no respite from guilt and poverty
Death-longing reborn in *forcados*.

Indifferent Los Arcos
cries over onions and cabbage
struggling too little against Fate,
Estella and Logrono borne better
your voice silenced by TV and hay market news
orphan antipasto in dowdy bar
your *alberges* run by pilgrim outsiders
your abbey rose garden a fragrant secret
ancient gravestones now cloister pavement
the common man outside, pissing on the soil.

You still say 'who cares?'
hardy farm folk occupying bars like glue
glass cabinet of *tapas* and *pinchos* sparse
Los Arcos bars of strangled fare
two pinchos, and take what's given
drinks the same, tardy indifference, sobering light.

Los Arcos tires of itself-
its indifference is tough, wheat-grained
winnowed in the *Calle Mayor*
ground indifference, ghosting over walls and arches

pilgrim fleeing your dark side streets
window mind's surly moderation
dour insularity, children running in circles
no-nonsense parents captive to dreamless nights.

Cry Los Arcos.
Let your tears savage the deserts.
Winch yourselves above the soil.
Know the plain that is forever yours.
Embrace the old town and all that might be.
Kiss the ladies, and join their dreams
of Love and Restoration.

6 From Triacastela
Galicia

Once over O'Cebreiro, its a long walk across the tops before the grand descent to little Triacastela.

From Tria

little grey matter by too little light
to pack, back and turn from our Tria nest.
step away to adore, stride-glide on foot
no carriage with Samos
my country boots for Sarria
with anonymous gosh
flit birds, hummm wheels
pilgrims met in silhouette
obsolete 'Bon Caminos'
given and taken
mad-glad my walk brought to
a standstill of thought

when here I am
moss veiled
the sun at my feet
and nowhere else
would I be
climbing the farm lane autumnal-
glade light, gleen sun
glad to be
uphill humble

and still...

still...

there's a path to Santiago
better still.

7 To San Domingo de la Calzada
La Rioja, Navarre

A tour guide's lonely work is assisting and supporting others 24 hours a day. Leading a walking group on the Spanish Camino de Santiago- far from home- I drive a minibus with other people's luggage, out-of-placeness my creeping enemy.

To San Domingo de la Calzada

Najera left, St Domingo de la Calzada imagined
fifteen minutes through vineyard and heath
mountains to the south
my walkers traversing Azofra and Ciranuela
undulating hours together
pilgrims caravans passing, almost
waving to my silent speedometer.

By curved hilltop picnic place, car butt aside
the Rioja on three horizons
I am unfree in all directions, standing
in midday's *sec* air
windless and fair for St Domingo on-the-plain
sandy, urban township
agri-framed, impasto mountains *verde*.

Imagine St Domingo in its Sunday best
white welcome to unmatched husbandry, plain view
distant mountains pressed to parallel lines
this traveler's heart not of this place
nor touched to the core.
Synapses snap;
in the great emptiness of Earth and sky
no-wonder.

Companions, where are you?
Deliver me; voice to me
touch and laugh over calamari
in-the-rib humour and casual asides.
Words jam in my throat until dusk
thoughts poised

pitch black, stagnant and bewitched
vacant before Rioja vineyard
being all south, and gone west.

Between earth and sky, over the fence sighting
ripe, dark grapes
conjuring desire
drawing me to help-myself.
Jump the fence. Kicking soft brown earth
straining skins in hand
clutching and tearing your crop farmer Juan
biting into your juicy grapes-
Bursting associations!
All the world made rich, nectar my body
engorge and satiate
ashen vision turning dark to thrill
blue to purple
Earth of birch, pine, oak and beech
winter snows falling in *Sistema Ibérico's*
softened rocks and hardening waters.

Look to those mountains again
eyes lifting two thousand metres.
I must go! I must go.
Not to the mountains today where
Griffon vultures hover over praying locals;
not to LaGuardia's fortified walls
nor Logrono's city delights
not to first friends found in *pensions*.

Drive on to St Domingo
sparkling like glass in sunshine
towering laughter to late lunches
roosters crowing
my strength bent against the shards of being.

* *Winner, Second, 2013 Glen Phillips Poetry Prize*

8   *Lost in Translation*

On first reading a translation of the *The Rooster and Hen Legend* in St Domingo de la Calzada, in the Spanish Rioja. **St Domingo de-la-Calzada** is a Riojan town of six thousand people. Part of the it's great winemaking region, the town is starkly divided into old and new town, twenty-two kilometres after Najera, and twenty-three before Belorado. For the walkers amongst us, it's an ideal distances for an easy day walk.

Welcome to Spain, the land of mystery, magic and the itchy, scratchy Rooster-and-Hen story, a fast and familiar pilgrim legend of unrequited love mixed with a little Rioja wine, all leading to wicked treachery.

Join our sunny St Domingo cafe lunch with its mouth-watering menu. We're reading the *Leyendes del Camino de Santiago*, a book-and-card set recounting this great medieval tale. Let us feast on its hapless English surrounded by seafood aromas, a jug of water and a plate of pickled vegetables, *sin costo*.

Our booklet opens with:

> *Willing to rest of the fatigue of the road, a marriage with their son stopped.*

A lovely sentence. It seems that our entre to the grand legend is one-short of a translator. So in the spirit of fraternity our preferred words might be: After a long day on the road, a couple and their son…

Continuing:

> *a marriage with their son stopped in a house in St Domingo de la Calzada.*

Ah-ha. The events took place here in San Domingo, perhaps in this very café.

> *The owner of the house had a daughter and she falls in love of the youth boy. But the boy did not correspond her, so she got revenge and she decides to accusing him of robbery.*

ie, propositioned by the young woman the dull, dull boy did not seize the moment, nor even 'correspond' her, obviously under his mother's thumb. Then:

> *Quickly the Justice catched the youth, after they found him with a glass that the girl did put inside him clothes, so he was hung.*

Hung? By the Justice? I feel for the boy. Our pious lad found out too late the cost and futility of rejecting a woman's advance.

I take a sip of water, and order wine. So far, it's a tragic story of sex verses piety, potent wine and portentous revenge, plainly an unfamiliar event in today's crowded pilgrim lodgings. Though events have moved fast, the story is very short of suspense. What happened between 'a glass that the girl she did put inside him' and 'he was hung'? Blinking missed it.

But my thoughts run ahead of me. I sip red wine and bite into the savory olives and pickles. The legend continues:

> *The parents felt, and continued their journey to Santiago de Compostela. When they come back for the same place the mother stopped for cry on the locus-in-quo he still continued hung.*

'Locus in quo' (I believe) means that after the hanging, the parent's long journey to Santiago continued, and when they returned found the nameless 'youth-boy' was still hinging there. Ick!

For all those who decry modern Justice's costs, procedures, slowness and outcomes, the Middle Ages are for you. No need for bureaucratic paperwork or due-process there. The 'justices' were not constrained by boring pros-and-cons of argument, evidence, doubts, contexts and fine judgments. If you're not from the right class or family, you're not a local or able to buy influence in the marketplace of ideas- you're dead. As such, medieval citizens missed out on the substance and dramatic positives of *LA Law*, *CSI*, *Cold Case* and *Rebus*, with their glorious cut and thrust, legal questioning, police interviews, the presentation of evidence, detective intuition, logic and inference, courtroom tactics and jury deliberations. In truth (and their ownership of this rare commodity), Church and gentry favoured summary and salutary justice, knowing that peasants were numerous, flawed and sometimes jumped to conclusions above their station. In days when Rome had more knocking shops than churches, and a succession of popes with some very bad habits, money bought

you so many Hail-Marys and a few indulgences to put things right. No need for *Sherlock Holmes, Morse, Frost, Poirot*, or even *Cluseau*. That lot only stirred up trouble.

But this is puzzling. What were the parent's motives in such behavior? The modern lawyer would have a field-day: 'So you two were so distressed seeing your son hung by the neck until dead, that you continued your holiday to Santiago de Compostela?' followed by 'With hindsight was your flagrant disregard for your son's fate the wisest possible course of action?'. And 'After such a gross injustice, was it piety that compelled you to continue your pilgrimage?' And 'Months later, you thought you'd receive a friendly reception when you returned to San Domingo?'

Sadly, the story offers no explanation. Apparently traveling to Santiago and back, over a thousand kilometres, finding their son still hanging from a tree, was to be expected- a shocking insight into medieval public health-and-safety.

Still, we are told that the parents:

> *stopped for cry on the locus-in-quo he still continued hung. When suddenly she listened of the youth's voice saying him that he continue with live thanks to that Santiago and the Virgin sustain him.*

It's a miracle. He's alive! Silly me. It seems the parent's pilgrimage has improved the boy's health. So:

> *Quickly their parents will see the judge. He was eating, when he heared the woman's story, the judge answered her that if their son was alive as the rooster and the roasted hen that he prepared to eat. At that moment, the birds returned suddenly to the life and they left flying off the table.*

Another miracle! I can't keep up. The humble parents find their boy alive after hanging for a month, and instead of returning him to their bosoms, they respectfully take the news to the presiding judge and plead restitution. And for their piety, this fellow anoints them with sarcasm and reason. And blow me down his chicken dinner comes to life and flies from the table.

I can hardly eat my meal now. Pigs might not fly of course, but we know chickens do. So it is only sensible that the arrogant judge gets his comeuppance. No way will this fellow humiliate the humble, pious mother, possibly named Mary. Clearly her powers of faith and obedience have revitalized the chickens, energizing them to grow feathers, stand and fly off the plate.

I take a deep breathe and find the courage to dig into my meal. 'Doing justice' to my calamari, *empanada*, a chicken and *ensalada platos* and a ham *bocadillo*, is an effort. But eventually my companions and I compare notes. We decide on our legend's strengths. Given the chickens and son are both resurrected, we reckon

-a good resurrection always gets attention

-the mother's touching faith is a kind of Medieval justice, as God knows the peasants weren't getting it anywhere else, and

-a judge eating two roasted chickens and a rooster is plain greedy.

Concluding our meal with more red wine, we sense that these miracles deserve a legendary denouement. So follows:

> *Astonished, the judge went where the boy was, and checking that he was alive, they returned him to his family then they took the birds to the church like test of the miracle.*

Having meted out abuse, treachery, arrogance and betrayal, the town judge then takes leave, replaced by the Church bishop. Of course he embraces the miracles as God's work, and neatly incorporates hens and rooster in the local church. Good trick.

But for those of us steeped in contemporary murder mysteries, so many questions remain. Was this story about betrayal and persecution of outsiders? Was it about an outsider's revenge on a greedy judge? How did they catch the rooster and chicken after the birds had flown? And if it was the judge who officiated (some dispute on this), why hand the birds to the Church when the judge could have eaten them twice? And where was the Bishop during this protracted dispute? The Church had extensive spy networks, and typically, knew everything under the sun (or thought they did). What happened to the innkeeper's daughter- free as a bird, flew the coop, or sent to a nunnery?

With our last sip of sweet, aromatic wine, our glasses have a swirling viscosity I hadn't noticed before.

Anyway, you can sense the sublime in this story. These medieval pilgrimages kept sinners worried, a good serving of miracles feeding the believer's faith. Even when the son was bewitched, betrayed, wrongly convicted and publicly hung, in the parent's heart-of-hearts, they realized that in cruelty, death and injustice there is Beauty.

Watching the afternoon sun quiver below the awning, and build gently sway in light, we draw our last tipsy, gypsy, dipsy conclusion, simply, that the youth boy the girl did put inside, continued pilgrimage by a hen and chicken, for the sun did speak, making judging hapless wonder translation true.

Let's get out of here.

St Domingo Cathedral Museum

9. The Meseta
A Photo Esssay

Between Burgos and Leon, we have a large expanse of low plateau famland. A pilgrim makes good distance eac day. If the weather is favourable, it offers great journey. Avoid high summer.

Fellow pilgrim in Sahagun, The Meseta.

Above: Festival, Leon. Below: Church, Fromista, Meseta.

Sahagun, between Burgos and Leon.

An eccentric house in Sahagun.

10

Astorga, Leon, north-west Spain.

To *Astorga*

Starting from **Leon**, a city of 135000 people, pilgrims need most of two days or tramp fifty-two kms. to reach Astorga. Sixteen kilometres beforehand, they cross *Hospital de Orbigo*'s crooked ancient bridge where a 'mad' knight challenged all-comers in jousts, apparently to win a woman's heart, and in the process, probably provided inspiration for Cervantes's Don Quixote.

A modest town of twelve thousand, Astorga has a Roman museum (the short film highly recommended), a *chocolateria*, old Roman walls, outdoor Roman archaeology, Pilgrim museum, cathedral, charming town square and Baroque town hall, an early Gaudi and a lively 'old town.' A poor pilgrim races through without taking in its delights, and a curious one will be torn by all its offerings. If you're hungry and brave, check out the *cocido maragato*, and visit the local bakeries, especially early in the morning.

Here are number of works written before Astorga:
* Feugo
* Proud Tortilla, followed by Pilgrim Astorga.

In my travel book, *Damn!* you find much more of my furious trials on this stretch.

Astorga, with the Cordillera Cantabrica behind.

Fuego   * Spanish for fire.

*F*uel highway,
ploughed land, furrowed brow
vibrating truck's overture to humming earth
and beating heart, my ground-weaving, expresso limp
two-step recital, indigo beat
corn-stalk staves waving to my unpacking day
compote aire, bracing arms
legs swinging, hill overcome, strike rhythm-
Astorga! Astorga!
and no one can stop me.

*N*oone can stop you,
arms, legs swinging
great good morning to
the *compote* aire, your unpacked daze,
waving to stave cornstalks
indigo beat, two-step recital,
the pillow clouds, the ploughed land
your furrowed brow
ground weaving, vibrating trucks
fueled for Astorga! Astorga!
highway Fuego.

Tortilla   *pronounced tor-tee-a

Proud tortilla, patata tale
the poet's novel yellow
baked-in words, a people's composition
puffed and partnered with bread, pepper
salad salacious, crown crisp
well spoken for.

Olive and garlic, earthy potato
and whipped eggs
memories of chickens pecking
cluck and puckery, the onion beside
Spanish villagers of yesterday
boundto
tomorrow's home.

11 *Pilgrim's Astorga*

Towards Astorga: one of my favorite larger town along the Camino Frances.

Bridge de Orbigo, 16 km before Astorga.

Pilgrims cross crooked Bridge de Orbigo

yesterday, today and tomorrow

imagine knight's battleground

a million morning's ago

Suero de Quiñones and his men

barred pilgrim's way, denying

'three hundred lances' in

legendary *camino* battles for a damsel's love;

*c*hivalrous clashes over dirt and stone
love and territory, vast arid plain unmoved

bloodied and brutal clash for honour and staving boredom.
Cervantes' Don Quixote, fool and fantasist
prone to farce and falsehood
taking food from people's mouths
for a 'higher' cause.

See Orbigo's cleaners, shopkeepers and drivers
peer down Calle Paso Honroso
torn between history and her story, voices mute
watching today's pilgrim parade
in clear air or miracle rain
grey eyes watch those bound for Astorga
snowy Cordillera Cantabria over their wintery shoulder.
Reach pilgrim Astorga, Roman fort of the nothing
late capital for little kingdoms,

hence abandoned and forlorn
unwanted by Asturians and Galicians alike
revived by soldiers of the camino, hostages to history
reclaimed by *La Maragatería* peoples
long memories of Astorian kings fighting Muslims
Galicians and Leonese; patrician Rome pressing meaning
blood here, grapes there, bred here
all the trappings of their engineering here;

slaves, sewerage and water works, baths and metal tools
barbs between rivals, each asking:

what ground do you cede?
who stands between you and slavery?

Like vellum wiped clean, Astorga is history rewritten
recovering dignity as stage of the pilgrimage
your *perigrinos*, thieves, farmers, shepherds
wives and soldiers eye each other in the wilderness;
homeliness won by persistent affections
overwhelm the mirage,

successive families gather in your town square
trade goods, display wares, dance in colourful costumes Baroque
town hall your finest audience
honoured in 'forever' stone
house worldly clock tower of man and woman
two figures dance to fixated time, slow-and-even waltzing; those
who have time, know time has them.

Astorga's people rise at dawn
sleep-walking to sweet and doughy bakeries
collect *pan de leche* and *rustico*, *tortilla* and *empanada* crusty as a
mountain, soft as a pillow;
the working woman's plain exterior
merges with austere skies stretching over the *meseta*.
With Roman, Asturian, pilgrim and saintly days
Astorga incants festivals four
citizens pray that they do not
    evaporate in Summer's sun.

    Ritual ceremony, icons and loud bands

conjure and banish the past, make you tradition-bound
illusion-maker, proffers security
snowflakes in a drought, burn cant and candles
no pleasing your devils, you say
'But we are Astorga, why bother us now
pregnant with ordinariness?'
even if Napoleon once came to Iberian Astorga
retreating after a text message from Josephine:
'Get yourself home Nap. Maybe Paris needs you.'

Happy pilgrims walk your daytime streets
visiting all the sites of your body
seeing your crown of Gaudi
your square and noble market face
your ignoble cathedral arms
worn, torn historical body with fortress walls around your
girth, ample stomach for café and restaurants of
extravagant, meaty meals
your moist and willing crutch
your people fond of laughter, tailored cuts for manly ways
bishop and shopkeepers urge formality and modesty
working people's clothing worn most days
intent on tasks as ordinary and mighty as your flanks.

By night Astorga is naked for delight
all fun and youthful bodies
bar stools pressed, local lights appeasing
hands kept clean for slow and hard
caressing eyes and mouths that will conspire

long the night, tall the spire
Astorga's crown put aside for royal duties
sisters, brothers, bishops, aunts and uncles
forgotten with your persistent aching
your man's chiselled face all passion and perspiration
giving yourself to the great unmaking
growing belly to another creation.

Restless pilgrim wakes dazzled, half-blinded
crazed and belly-full of wine bar night.
Find your way onto the rising plain
Molinaseca two days thanks, remind yourself
that pilgrim dreams are won by doing.
Your morning is dark, and full of muffled whisperings
crinkled plastics, snores, and metal scrapping.

Alive to sound, you ease yourself into being
fingers running along numb walls, toes cold and alive
gathering your wits from the echoing light
clothes drying in one-euro cupboards.
Try walking down stairs, brush your teeth badly
shampoo in the shower whilst counting money
saying fond farewells to those still sleeping.
Get value-for-money by drinking three coffees
roast the toast, do the post, and conspire
in three Latin languages.

The morning chill hits your fresh face.
Load your donkey-self, retire the bill
full silence and a hug for one's awake

hand to the door
depart Astorga's last embrace.
Keep your eyes afore lest you recall too much of late.

Yellow arrows show the way.
Beat your staff upon ceramic floors
stride the laneways for Astorga's last word on love:
the baker's light outshines the morbid mist-
eyes falling on crusty breads, *churros*, sweets
and custardy pastries you admire,

Astorga's cleaners, teachers, landlords
wives and children of the morning
bid you fond farewell.
With Astorgan memories in your pack
accepting the clock strikes seven
your eyes fix on the road ahead
bread between you teeth, map in hand,
passion renewed
no time for chivalrous knights.
Your horizon eyes see tomorrow
your weary legs, only today.

12 Like a Bird

Like a Bird

Like the bird I am
crane white, black foot
call me higher than church
taller than bishops
per apse majestic
protected by law
nested in sticks
towering
air-conditioned I sing
notes of semi-quaver.
Once crochetty in Piccadilly
I have flown to the meseta
where choirs warm my eggs
and organs make me dance.

13 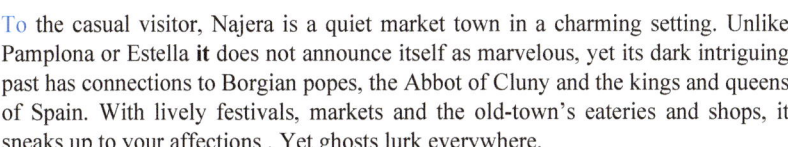 *Marvelous Najera*

To the casual visitor, Najera is a quiet market town in a charming setting. Unlike Pamplona or Estella **it** does not announce itself as marvelous, yet its dark intriguing past has connections to Borgian popes, the Abbot of Cluny and the kings and queens of Spain. With lively festivals, markets and the old-town's eateries and shops, it sneaks up to your affections . Yet ghosts lurk everywhere.

Najera, pronounced NA-hera, is the former capital of all Navarre, in earliest times a place of caves, wildlife, forest and mountain springs, a little paradise for first peoples, later becoming bountiful agricultural land attracting Celts, Romans, Visigoths, Muslims and hermits.

Najera means 'town between the cliff', a natural frontier for conflict and ideas, possessed by Christian and Muslim, caught between the hard rocks of rival kingdoms- Pamplona, Navarre, Burgos, Castille and Asturias, flows through centuries as a family name, one musician Najerian caught between clefts.

From Mont de la Demande in the south, Rio Najerrilla flows into you. From 1032, your young village was honoured by grand church, monastery and crypt, becomes last home for thirty querulous kings and queens. Each begged for proximity to the Black Virgin's shrine, in your cliff cave enfolded by your cathedral, the Virgin magically appearing before King Don Garcia- you deceiver and rogue- thinking you had cemented your authority by miracles and piety of appearance. No luck, no charm, Don Garcia.

You were soon at war with your brother, winner takes all, calamitous Battle of Altapuerca (1054) seeing Najera disavowed, waters flowing, spared ignominy by surrounding monasteries, landlords and first keepers of the Spanish language, Tradition a staunch and bloody barrier to Saracens and peasant revolts. Like Albi to the north, your church was built as fortress, the Camino de Santiago routed here, a Christian line-in-the-sand, drawn, and never to be crossed.

Abbot of Cluny, Peter the Venerable favoured you, meeting his translators here in 1142, commissions the Qur'an written in a European language, first time. Later, Rodrigo Borgia (later Pope Alexander) funded your reconstruction, a new clothing of honour and prestige.

The One-Hundred Year War found you, waters flowing, sixty-thousand Franco-Castilians battling twenty-four thousand Anglo-Gascon force at Naverette, later crash into town (1367), English longbows prevailing. Arrows over your head Najera. And even when your enemy was vanquished, time and money were the only winners.

In Spain's tumultuous, debt-ridden times, you were no refuge. Your vacillating nineteenth century Queen Isabella II brought disaster and decolonization, your privileged monasteries befouled, confiscated and sold, warring parties kept prisoner in your abbey and cloister, a desperate prisoner inscribing 'INOCENT' on your door. In an age of raw injustice, courage become your greatest value, outrage your passion, disappointments taken out on bulls.

> Today's innocent pilgrims
>
> pass homely doors and empty shops
>
> footpaths fade, parkland marriage to
>
> parking slots and waiting-square
>
> sometimes-busy markets, corner nooks
>
> to Chinese chow-min
>
> butcher and baker stand-in sunshine
>
> awaiting customers. Thirsty pilgrims take refuge
>
> in old-town's pensions and alberges
>
> under denuded cliffs, by crumbling lanes
>
> and artless gates.
>
> In cafes and bars, shell-bearers
>
> seek soft cakes and fair exchange
>
> barred from hermit caves by

archaeologists posting signs saying
'Geography tells no lies', as only they
see the ancestors laugh and weep.

Innocent-of-irony walkers depart next day
for Azofra and St Domingo
no time for monastery, museum or curiosity
they rediscover their pilgrimage to speed.
Yet one pilgrim seized by moon madness
sneaks into church and monastery by night
search for your soul.

Crazed for time, she
circles the cloister of the caballeros
built for inner reflection, cross-hairs open to sky.
Her stark self sees stars where others found
calendars for agriculture, guidebooks for navigation
tales of antiquity and the loneliness of Man
Romanesque columns lifting
stone floors and paths underline
the taunting heavens.

Pass stone carvings of the guilty pleasures-
music, flesh and fighting-
denied to monks and nuns (or so it is said)
she serves at the table where
nuns pick at their chastity
fondle their poverty and wrestle with words;
priests wrestle with chastity
pick at poverty and fondle their words.

Inside her cavernous church
handsome chest of a thousand carvings
sculpted to excess
Adam and Eve naked to gold and silver
Riojan grapes blood's adornment
reconciling nuns and monks to themselves;
they are landlords, and friends of the mighty.
Outside, the peasants starve.

Her scorching eyes and handsome brow see
choir chairs enchanting, comic and fantastic
designs of intertwined 'F' and 'I'
for Ferdinand and Isabella
King and Queen of first Spain
carved heart of, a drop of blood spilt
symbol of the broken hearts of ninety-two
twin towers of Jewish expulsion and
Columbus discovers India.

When night becomes morning, she tunnels
to the mausoleum of pale stones
where omens, angels and devils were
once grand ideas
past hair column and tonsure arch
where the candles burn
her Black Madonna whispers
that Nature is lost in this womb of time.

Pilgrim flight between her cliff and cleft
heartbeat to the babble *Najerrilla*

where ice nocturnes the grasses
white van passes over the viola bridge
bakers work in morning tempo
the stars hitch to companion time.

It's coffee for Our Lady the shaken traveler
ever bewitched by Najera's ways
while locals dream pilgrims flowing like water
alberges fill and empty the day
shell-travelers mind their own business after all.

The mysterious Black Virgin icon.

Giant Songbook for choirs. Los Arco

14 These Birds Have Flown

St Domingo de la Calzada, Rioja, Northern Spain.

These Birds Have Flown

Arriving in St Domingo an hour before my intrepid walkers, I know they'll be tired and hungry so I've bought food for a late lunch. As a tour guide I know St Domingo de la Calzada as a special town, and not just for its long name, de-la-Calzada, meaning of-the-road, that is, on the way to Santiago de Compostela.

St Domingo's old walled city's street and buildings are largely preserved after many centuries. It has a prestigious cathedral and several museums. But that's not the feature I am determined to show my guests. Nor is it the charming town square with its lofty Eighteenth century tower over my shoulder, so massive that it collapsed under its weight and had to be rebuilt.

By the time my group gathers in the old square, I ready, pointing to a massive cathedral door that appears unused, dusty and locked.

'Before we lunch, let's quickly visit the cathedral. You'll never see the likes of it again. It's the rooster-and-hen miracle.'

My gang looks puzzled, last night's recital of the legend already forgotten. The hapless cartoon guidebook translation was damn funny, but the tale of a hung young man coming to life months later after being suspended from a tree was the stuff of miracles and mirth. Perhaps my pilgrims were just too hungry or tired after their long day's walk. But I remind them that the parents, seeing the miracle of their long dead son talking to them, appealed for clemency from the 'justice' who mocked their miracle, only to see his two roast chickens fly off the table.

Pointing again to a massive cathedral door, 'It's just over there. You remember the legend? The miracle of the rooster and hen? When the Governor's roast chickens flew away?'

Recognition dawns. There's reduced enthusiasm for history and mythology at a time like this, but I am keen to display my own piece of wonder through the heavily disguised cathedral door.

'We can photograph the world's only rooster housed in a cathedral,' I declare. Photo opportunity! Interest reincarnated.

One problem. I can't leave our lunch sitting in the old town square for the next ten minutes lest it fly away or be eaten by cats, so I pack most of it in my daypack, the rest on my body.

Strolling to the massive cathedral doors, everyone sees that they are closed, locked and bolted. There's a sign directing people to the museum around the corner where they will charge an entrance fee. This is my moment. Grabbing a small handle, I open a hatch and climb through.

'Come on.'

They rush forward, and stoop to enter. Inside is a sign with a litany of rules and restrictions, written in Spanish, saying...

'It's OK.'

I know the rules, or at least, the most likely ones. Number one: silence. Very important. Keep the noise down- that sort of thing. And don't worry too much about that symbolic camera with a cross over it.

As our eyes adjust to the dim light. We take in the stone flooring, the overbearing institutional structures and their decorative elements, eventually realise that we are hemmed-in by metre-high barriers- 'corralled' as Americans would say, or cooped-up, as an Australian might say. Beyond our enclosure is some unknown domain, probably the museum.

'Go no further', said a deep voice from the darkness- probably God's.

'It's OK.' I reassure my intimidated ones, 'The hen house is nearby,' at the time disorientated and surprised. It was not as I had recalled it when I first discovered it. It was as if someone had completely rearranged it. Where were the roosters?

And looking up- 'Here. Here it is.'

High above its ornate stone base was the chicken-chapel with its ornate columns, a dark wooden gallery, seamlessly integrated into the stone walls, a gilded cage less than two metres wide and perhaps the same height. We peer determinedly, gawking at the barred windows without spying any wild life. We gawk some more. Where are the roosters and hens?

We stare upwards at the high altar, Sure enough; we can soon make out the birds- a rooster, and a few chickens parade past the bars. This is a church, right? And they keep roosters and hens indoors.

This time I'm taking photos. Others too reach for their cameras, when someone unfortunate points to the sign of a camera with a cross on it.

'It's OK,' I say, 'No flash.'

And so, cameras in hand, we harvest our visuals before preparing for retreat. My accomplices gather around. We have the forbidden images - our less-then-original sin. Taking up positions, we ready for escape into the bright light of innocence. Hugging my forbidden daypack with its warm food against my chest, I have our lunch of two roast chickens.

Eek! Two roast chickens, held against my body- roasted and barbequed. Trespass. We must fly.

I crouch at the hatch like the hunchback of Notre Dame, remember the young lad of the legend, hung for stealing a glass from the innkeeper. The guards list my crimes: forbidden photos, entering with food, verboten backpacks - and stealing the sacred chickens. Capital offense.

15   *Cordillera Cantabrica*

High Cordillera Cantabrica, Manjarin and Acebo. Pilgrims leaving Astorga, rise steadily for **Foncebadon** and Cruz de Ferro. Soon after, they start a slow descent from high **Manjarin** and **Acebo**, before a steeper descent to **Molinaseca**. All the way they straddle the Cordilara Cantabrica, a sleeping giant, our travelers barely noticing until rapid changing weather strikes.

On Cordillera Cantabrica

Cordillera Cantabrica- you are wild sierra after Astorga, ramparts to colder climes, your pilgrim pole peaking at border to the Beirzo, once doorway to Galicia, tall Cruz de Ferro wrapped in rags, young admirers blessing you like true primitives, arriving by foot or pedal like colourful storks on the mound, your high pass, taut and muscular, helmet prophylactics- whatever is tall must be round, men and women leaving messages at your base in twenty languages, hairpins, ribbons and socks, only a stones throw from hippy **Mandarin** and cowboy **Acebo**, like movie sets, pilgrims stride, stroll or lumber with unmistakable illusions in their backpacks, getting lighter with every day.

You are mountain my cordillera, higher than Roncesvalles in the Pyrenees, pilgrims panting, bearing water for Spain and Portugal, made of rift valleys and grassy plains. Your grasses

Manjarin

attract shepherds, milkmen and scoundrels, wild Beirzo content with splendid isolation, black sheep to brother Galicians and Astorians. Your sky conjures winds and lightning, hail and snow, rain and sleet, blowing pilgrims from finger paths to shoulder towns.

Past Ferro, Manjarin is a primitive abode, glad signs for Jerusalem, Trondheim, Machu Pichu, Santiago, flags flown, laughter in ruins, aching in your bones, you stay overnight, joking to the mist and snow, kept warm by teapots, fire place and borrowed sanity, like a treasured library where you can always borrow time.

Manjarin's Tomas and Jose- population two- ring bells in the mists, welcome pilgrims like mythic days of old, take care of injuries, making memories to the strains of Gregorian chant, twenty-five beds awaiting pilgrim slumber, under roof and attic. Knights Templar in mind, pilgrims given warm mushrooms and couscous, cook up a hug, bank on snows that once swallowed the town, abandoned to the mists and rain and ice sees it's hand extended, candles for light, teapots as juggernaut. Even mountains shiver.

Further from Jerusalem is one-goat **Acebo**, built on your slopes, of wood, string, and stone, lodgings guarded by bearded goat and gunslinger eyes, doors closed to sunshine, showdown street with mysterious corners into the abyss, silence air shattered by Coke dispenser and walking sticks, matter-of-fact pilgrims drinking coffee, bearing bread and fruit, doorstop pandemonium when dogs take exception to a catty promenade. Its *albergue* is saviour in foul weather, its attic beds notorious, breakfast is food for the spirit, and Hope is the orange juice's secret ingredient.

Cordillera sings for pilgrims, whistles, insteps and swing, yodels and croons, your delirious, frozen breath, a wolverine wind, chilly welcome to Acebo's solitary square, pilgrims spotting the lower church and emu-tree. Pilgrim companions, jolly to the wind, patient in bearing, rub their cheeks, pull down their hat before pack water bottles and lift themselves higher than Everest - Molinaseca below.

Hours later, feel warm air beats around their ears on dry heath hillsides, pleasure and surprise after Astorga's long plain and Cordillera Cantabria's icy winds. Laughable Acebo and Manjarin is far behind our sinuous, curvaceous path into this vale of warmth, seeing a first mountain stream for donkey's ages, green-grey mane flowing beneath its ancient bridge, pilgrims passing beneath disbelief's yellow skies, a pebbly beach, swimmers loving the sun, children chasing birds, roaring waters drawing breath, caressing airs and a shimmering pool; pilgrim's first stop, the door inn.

Oasis Molinaseca is a mall and compact village, taverna of warmth and decoration, menus and hubbub, fellow pilgrims gathering to feast on interiors, neighbouring Spanish day walkers toasting victory over Bridges of Malpaso.

At the foot of Cordillera, see your stone paths and narrow streets of solid yesterday. your town planted between river and mountain slopes, first for pilgrims, urban and urbane, promising all delights, commerce for the unrobbed, compassion for survivors. Upstairs Acebo and Manjarin still linger to mind: they made you a pilgrim.

Looking past Acebo. towards Molinaseca. Below, Signs at Marjarin.

Messages left around the Cruz de Ferro.

16 The magnificent Garganta day walk in Picos d'Europa

Off the camino del Norte, and some ninety km north of Leon, Picos d'Europa's limestone mountains, jutting out behind the Bay of Biscay, is special place, the Garganta day walk one of the best.

Garganta Walk, Picos d'Europa.

Garganta Track, Picos.

17   Tribute to Arzua

Arzua is a Galician market town, forty k. (or twenty-six miles) from Santiago de Compostela. It's a 'last post' before the pilgrim's big-push into Santiago.
Many pilgrims think Arzua 'grey', although plainly convenient as an overnight stay. Slightly smaller than Melide fifteen kilometres earlier, it has a dozen accommodation places including further refugios and alberges before and after town. Although it has few ancient heritage sites, its architectural heritage modest, Arzua offers something less tangible and easily missed by the single-minded.'

Tribute to Arzua

Weary pilgrims enter Galician Arzua
walk its marrow lanes in lime light
expectant minds fixed on tomorrow, or the day after,
journey's end grand Santiago de Compostela.

After long day's walk through eucalypt forest,
past red-roofed farmhouse and hórreo,
they are mustard for beds, shower and meals,
Arzua's white buildings, thumping trucks
and burly white vans, the dispiriting rhythm of the ordinary.

In evening park, under tree and sculpture
passers-by carry white shopping bags,
children display, ellipse conversations,
a lone pilgrim with jamon, gesso and bread
reads besides two-legged, cement heroes in boots-
not Gods, saints, Franco or Guard Civile,

but a peasant couple hauling two cows
bumping against pilgrim paragraph,

man and woman press bovine flanks,
she pulls a beast's tail, he turns a cow's head
en force, twelve legs upstanding,
with cows facing opposite directions
park visitors never confronted by two bos backsides.

Literature's eyes put aside, our pilgrim
spies autumnal leaves on wet bronze
                reaches
                                    touches
a float film of dust and oils, alchemy for bronze.

Her quivering reflection quavers revelation:
Arzua is of oil and dust,
agriculture and earthy commerce,
seven-thousand souls accept stray shorthorn
and the enchanted ones who wonder your back lanes,
follow the Milky Way.

Your sculpture speaks of that round-and-round world
of the doing,
hard days hauling the Rubia Gallega,
Frisian and Alpine Browns,
standing in their muck,
opening and closing gates,
on foot, everyone knowing The Way,
townspeople and pilgrim separated
by a thin veil of dreams.

Enchanted at the feet of farmer and bovine,
she confesses:
I dreamt abbeys, saints, cathedrals and mountain kings,
Santiago beckoning.
While we pilgrims walk the world of gramp ideas
your two cows and to people
speak plain and well
of sensuality, commerce and community.

Clever artisan
embodies the dignity of work,
the dignity of view,

people clutching those endearing animals,
perfect picture of fraternity,
of roundness and affection,
reassuring toughness, seductive continuity.

She declares:
Santiago pilgrim parties pale-
you Arzua, are better journey's end.

18 From *Palas de Rey*

Building
Also as Song. From Palas de Rei, Galicia, Spain

Palas crops and gardens the passing years
in building gaps
bloom and blossom stemming drear
to landed owner's songs of gloom
the ghosts of rooms between
plants of garden, people harden
passing near.

Through the sap and gap of days
weeds and fungi hold fast the locks
abandoned smock and broken chair
to carpet night, darkness times
the fevered lovers entwined as vines
to plants of garden, plants of pardon
tender near.

Another block, another clock, another fear
twisted roads, leering lanes known by ear
builders turn the bleeding soil with spades and hearts
planting seed for next the diamond days
to plants of garden, plants of pardon
lime and lemon harvest near.

Conceding folly, town so jolly when pilgrims here
bodies, packs and lasting shells sincere
to alberge heating, rise and fall the mugs of beer
children playing Tomorrow riding near
plants of pardon, plants of garden
building here.

Palas crops and gardens the passing years.

19   *Drive-by Hooting*

Santiago de Compostela tour bus drivers are tested, as this demented soul knows.

Drive-by Hooting

It's heading towards me
the driver seeing everything-
strips of light, dark pools, reflective surfaces
oil slicks, moving feet, brown wet blur
dashboard curd and needles, screaming yellow
fleeting objects- and hazy me.

Past dashboard
through windscreen
over engine and bumper beyond
there's driving rain, and little protection-
iron and chrome have ways of entering your life
flash, bang, crunch and grind before everything goes black.

Or else ears pegged
eyes like spears, foot poised
fearing
advertising hoardings fleeting poles
glinting,blind, blank and bewildered
repproaching Santiago de Compostela.

Drive-by hooting!

I'd kill to be in a cosy room, a lively restaurant
but right now
hooting must do
my Camino is round and around the walled-city
a million lost pilgrim prayers gladly accepted.

Could 'lose it' at any moment
Can't go
here or there
or forward or...opps!
My camino trails to nil, wagon
caught in hospital car park.

Back up.
Squeeze past.
Watch that car. Easy. Easy.
'You go first.' Hoot. Hoot.

In the narrows, the sign says...
think it says...
so it's OK isn't it?
'Between the hours of...'
think it says- this and 4pm.
Not three yet. What comes around goes...
Skirt the outlying banner, miss that child
squeeze past those people in brown.
What a shop, eh? *Not now!*
I've people to meet, bags to unload,
time ticks, destination two blocks away.
Two millimetres mental fuse.
Drive-by hooting.

The hotel down that lane? There! Go. Go.
Aim for the front door, gate open
and sometimes not.
the sign says something like, well
says something, like 'closed from... to...'
But it's open now!
Here goes.

Narrow.
Down street
tight
numerous
impediments
this hapless driver

swings off
the old road, into the lane
squeezing past the iron-gate.
Right-hand vision impossible.

Can't see a bloody thing.
Up above, cables loop down.
Street lights scrawny heads
out of crusty buildings.
Scratching my head
walls both sides
street as
pedestrian walkway
with shopfronts
and
outdoor seating.
Squeeze
past happy tourists
perched below my right
wheel.

This is it.
All my troubles over?
Who cares! Get it done, and Go. Go.

Drop-off completed
exit the old town before gates lock again.
Find a parking space within one kilometre-
just a matter of squeezing around tight corners
without demolishing the neighbours;
just a matter of finding parking in a car-crazy town;
a matter of floating on twlight, crinkling space until
the birds know it's time to fly.

Hold your horsepower.
I'm a drive-by hooter.

Farewell Santiago

Farewell Santiago, misty November
riding by the bones of your rail
hills of white, allegorical buildings
to my underground pages
history's ages, found farm and pasture
sombre broach to dipsy lanes
sweet pilgrims given welcome
by reliquary, Santiago commerce
knowing its place
as we too, too often forget
to love
the ones we're with.

Farewell Santiago
you were never my end
religious accent withstanding
Arzua's psalms
all ways Camino from Leon
lost-and-found pilgrims bear
bocadillos and staff
cross-country travelers eye the *cordillero*
Cacabelos near
Sarria sound
and sore feet too, too often
remember
the cherished ones of home.

Farewell Santiago
farewell.

Other Spanish Destinations: Segovia & Basque Country

A focus on Bermeo on the Bay of Biscay and Segovia, the old capital north of Madrid is inevitable, given they present their own attractions and inspiration.

Bermeo has been a Basque fishing port for seemingly all time, a town largely in the shadow of nearby **Guernika** and **Bilbao**. It is a quintessential Basque town who identity is sown into it soul.

Segovia is so different, with it deep links to the Spanish and Roman history. A cluster of heritage, history and architecture so compact that only walking around can possibly do it justice. Amongst its lesser known treasures is an ancient, public garden, used to feed its poor and less fortunate since the Seventeenth century, it water mills that drove Spanish first mint.

San Sebastian

Tribute to Bermeo

Style is knowing who you are, what you want to say, and not giving a damn. Gore Vidal.

Bermeo, Bermeo,
passion and sorrow beneath your forest blanket.

On steep and wooded coast, arena to the Bay of Biscay,
Bermeo, home and hearth around a small inlet,
your tall apartments hug slopes like eager spectators,
residents drink morning coffee from balconies,
your children play, overlook harbour and mighty sea walls.

The incoming sea-craft dock their catch,
bob on reverberating waters,
bounce off disappointments,
point to persistent centuries of struggle
against the rambunctious sea,
eyes drawn to the horizon,
where dwells the souls of fisher folk lost.

First train steels your heart,
burrows into its station.
People walk through turnstiles,
pass cast-iron barriers and dark gates,
white signs in your fond language,
loud air, closed faces,
a morning pedestrian with the sun in her eyes
whispers to the day 'Something might come of it.'

Residents in the old town apartments,
lo0k from their windows and balconies
across narrow lanes, see neighbours hang their washing,

search for brothers, sisters and bread.
Men and women make love on ample beds
in small rooms, watch television, cream on their lips,
with his manly touch, she whispers
'Something came of that.'

2.
In the park: bandstand, footpaths, patterned garden,
lush lawn and cast-iron seats,
older men and women chat,
play cards and watch the future pass,
cafes and eateries surround-
basic menus, princely banners, waiters scurry;

by the ONCE booth where
townspeople buy lottery tickets, draw on luck
in hope of the big win,
children ride small bicycles and scooters,
mother's earnest watch, raised eyebrows to new arrivals.
Check tickets again- no big win today.

Sing yesterday
when fires burnt your wood foundations,
rebuilt over successive centuries until
today's stone and brick things
cling to your rocky shores,
like limpets, mussels and periwinkles.
Tides wash in and out, crabs move sideways;
sensing a tsunami, patrons climb stairs,
coffee cups still in their hands.

You know who you are Bermeo.
Your fit young men in white trousers and shirts
promenade the afternoon sun
with brothers, sisters and mothers,
a white bandage of honour

wrapped around their wrist for all to see.
Like a detective or spy, a stranger might follow,
see them disappear into a large building of iron,
dark windows no telling sign in a stranger's mind,
when everyone else knows its name.

Basque Pelote- a Pelote arena.
Not tennis- hitting the ball over a net with elegant racket-
Pelote. the ball hit against walls
with bare hands or leather glove,
courts appearing in Spain and France
something like knowing you're in Basque country.

Tell them you are a winner Bermeo,
that you have style Bermeo,
knowing the Basque beret (txapela) is a trophy,
the word for champion, txapeldun,
the one who has a beret.

3.
Iron-in-rock Bermeo,
concrete promenade under foot,
sunburnt homes carved from the forest
taken from you by fire:
the fire of guns, of conquest and carelessness,
the fire of gas for meals, dreams and nightmares,
at last, your offshore gas fields moored to dreams.

Now climb the harbour steps to a metallic woman,
hand to her lips in desperate search for
men, boys and husband's safe return from the sea's clutches
with a fine catch in boats of colour,
or else drowned, attacked and forever sunk from view,
made grieving parent or widow with children distressed.

Behind the station, a locked cathedral and ancient abbey,
weeds at their feet, eighteen-thousand resilient people
walk indifferent past the fourteenth century
to apartments over piety
lost forever to twentieth century guns and bombs
of catholic Franco and fascist Hitler.

Stone-on-stone Bermeo,
Ercilla Tower, last of thirty to your walled city,
three floors holding centurion memories of fisher people,
trade unionists, poets and wealthy gentlemen,
strange bedfellows of finance and fraternity,
uneasy relations,
sullen against your eighteenth-century town hall,

elegant new dress paraded to your central square.

Around the corner,
barnacle shops and storehouses cling to rocky shore,
café tables, seaside crags, stairs to somewhere,
people washed over by the sea, earnest and grim,
tortilla under fork, worry and promise in their eyes.

They remember sister Guernica,
pummelled and plundered by Hitler's warplanes,
Basque nation trembling on still-born independence,
when Bermeo fought the Battle of Machichaco,
against the odds, four small trawlers protected
Republican people, guns and coinage
against the rebel cruiser *Canarias*,
sea-green fish nets against carnivorous cannon.

Thirty-six dead stand high on the hill,
a nickel sculpture for their loss, our loss,
remembering all that was broken and sunk,
and all that has been floated again-
Battle of Machichaco,
your trawlers destroyed or damaged,
Nature's salute is the crags offshore,
built of shipwrecks.

4.
Festival approaches.
Your men hover around gas bottles
for BBQ celebrations in the park,
fairground trappings of sweets, games and contest,
national flags flown high on balconies.

A weightless man clings to a hundred colourful balloons

begging us to buy before he floats away.
Technicians wrestle stage wires,
test lights and puffing fog.
Jeweller and fortune-teller offer beauty and hope.

In lengthening port shadow, high street's procession
led by a tall grotesque, thin man in indigo-blue,
wooden face with horsehair mane.

Man-on-stilts leans with cold accusative eyes,
lurch one way, then another,
unpredictable and frightening, like the centuries.

The crowd applauds young women in folk dress,
hears a single drum beat, a silent note,
repeat, repeat,
sombre, militant, foreboding,
as restrained as a funeral.

Mothers and grandmothers follow,
the elder women hold dolls, pride of tomorrow.
Cooks and medicos present,
again with drums,
again the missing, heart-stopping note
of past and future sorrow.

Men in black berets and steel-blue shirts
with white scarves of honour
are pictures of manly strength,
march to the same beat, the same sorrow,
declaring readiness for tomorrow's courage.

Precious Bermeo;
all that you have Bermeo,
Basque Bermeo,
and all that you might be,
passion and sorrow neath your forest blanket.

Bermeo, day of the festival and procession.

Above, the author in Bermeo. Below, Bermeo public building.

22   SEGOVIA GALLERY

Segovia, the old capital. Everything is within easy walking distance.

Lower Segovia is marked ancient food gardens, water channels, mills and machinery for Spain's first mint, below.

Sleep

Sleep is rust red
earthen, underground
mining-the-cranium
antediluvian yesterday.
Jung enough?
Mind-hazy diggg
kick ground
extract yesterday's fear
dumped in your backyard
smoulderunes;
today's homes built for
sleep's good work.

Compendium to **Damn!**

Leon to Santiago

In my travel book ***Damn!*** my solo, three hundred kilometre walk started or more accurately, staggered, from Leon, place to place in crisis or distress. However I was determined to reach Santiago de Compostela, along the way demanding of myself stories and poetica.

While long-distance walking is my spiritual pursuit, so too were the people and place met. With my other focus on creative work, in *Damn!* I recall how various poetica were first imagined and composed, ie, the story behind the story. Some of the work are found in full earlier in this book, but most are not. So here are the others.

Festival, Pont de Lima.

23 *Portomarin*

Portomarin was an ancient town built beside the old Roman bridge over the Mino River. In the 1960s, old town was uprooted to make way for the Belesar Reservoir. Its castle-style Church of San Juan was dismantled and rebuilt on the nearby hill, the new grid town built on a hillside. The town is uncomfortable with itself, a grid imposed on a hillside. It is 'all uphill', so I have never stayed there. Even on the last occasion, I walked on to **Gonzar**.

To Portomarin*

From teahouse peak, rollercoaster ride
besides gorse, because
Portomarin moved from time to time
underwater cause, applause missing,
their town drowned,
turned back men and women
mourn the dam to damn hours
by Helculean estate.

By damned tears, women's gaze
a cause for men's applause
from time to time,
Portomarin moved to gorse hill,
rollercoaster ride
history's teahouse hilt to hill,
stones journey's dismay,
construction cathedral below measure.

Pilgrims walk over hollow hill,
the missing buried 'neath tears,
arrivals beer-friendly,
wayfarers waving, cafe applause
spare ribs and limbs at source,
Portomarin's pilgrim people turned away
all regret, no doubt, stride away
Gonzar bound.

*Portomarin is a Galician town on the pilgrimage route to Santiago de Compostela, Spain.

24 *Let Me Die*

Let me die.

Are these the words of a tragic Shakespearian king, an Allepo father after losing his wife and children, or perhaps an agonized Tennessee William's character? Could be. But they are my own, after a monumental climb up steep track in drenching rain and cold, to O'Cebreiro, the official entry point into the Province of Galicia in Northern Spain.

It had rained all night, Daylight would not be evident until nine- and the last *pastelera* was behind me. Despair!

I had a simple breakfast of coffee and cake, loaded up, stepped out, walking in darkness, barely able to follow the painted yellow arrows bound for Mecca. After the first eight kilometres steady climbing, I was suffering. But my plan was intact: walk a short day with an early start, arrive in O'Cebreiro around noon, keeping dry with my highly-strung umbrella for protection.

The usual parade of cafes, bars and eateries typical of the pilgrim route were either closed or non-existent this morning. Only green pastures, drenched forest and rippling, gushing waters sustained me. I had passed a few walkers with torchlight, and one after other passed me in the dark. None of them looked happy.

Though well prepared, the steepening climb toyed with my self-assurance. With too many layers of clothes, my body was overheating, making me sweat profusely. It 'rained' under the clothing, and I could no longer keep up with my casual walking partner, a lanky Dutchman I had met a few kilometres back.

So I let him continue ahead while I flagged, eventually pulling-up a lonely hillside stop in downpours with wind gusts harrying my umbrella. I removed my woolen jumper and neckerchief. before continuing the long climb to a single solitary eatery without any certainty it would be open this late in the year. The climb never seemed to end. The torment.

Seeing 'one kilometre' painted on the tarmac- A stopping place? And later, '500m.' An after what seemed like another hour, there! Once through the door, I threw off my pack and ordered a large beer. Yep- after all that rain, chilly air, cloud and mist, all those *cafe con leches* dreams, I ordered beer.

Later I had toast and two oily fried eggs, the best I've ever tasted. Were my taste buds 'honest' or deceiving me? Come to think of it, beer, eggs and toast, coffee and cake might not be the best food combination.

Then, the final push to the celebrated O'Cebreiro with its ancient church and a dozen alberges, bars and eateries built exclusively for the quarter million people passing through each year. The rain continued. On the cross pasture farm track, the mud and water offered more delights on a clouded mountaintop. Grabbed a Coke. Sought out a warm cavern for coffee and food. Drawn to a smoky aroma, I entered the Meson-Something-or-Another wondering whether it was a warming fireplace or the aromas of smoky Galician sausages sizzling in a pan. And lo! There was a fireplace with ten pilgrims nearby, their wet weather gear and umbrellas left by the door, sitting at a plain bench-top slurping the house-made garlic *sopa*.

'*Sopa, par favor*,' I said.

With the large pot nearby, the bar woman ladled the soup into the bowl and served it on a traditional Galician wood platter. A group of Spaniards entered just as I start eating.

'*Sopa, par favor.*'

They crowded around the bar. I moved my elbows in, huddling over my precious sopa. The first taste was a knockout. Thick but not dense, it had mainly potato, chick peas, cabbage, a green-leafed vegetable and garlic, plenty of it. I savoured it knowing the platter could be used as a lid to keep it warm for up to an hour.

Fifteen minutes later, I was seized by nausea. My stomach was upside down. My heart sank. My brain seized up. I was overwhelmed and sickened, my consciousness wavering. Is it a heart attack? Indigestion? Will I vomit? Seeing the swirling mist beyond the open door only made matters worse. I was overcome with exhaustion and stomach trouble. Let me Die!
Later, I found an uneasy equilibrium. The nausea had eased but the Meson-Something-or-Another had lost its appeal. I'll walk to the next alberge. Another six k won't hurt; it might help.

And it did at first. Reaching the new, mountaintop municipal *alberge* I was impressed by a pleasant view from thirteen hundred metres altitude. Inside it had a modern heating system, washing facilities and most mod cons. I paid the six euros, discovering soon after- eek- there is no wi-fi. But worse, it did not provide blankets. What was I supposed to sleep in, my clothes?

So I left it on less than happy terms, loaded up and stepped back into the rain and mist. This was not good. It was not 'the plan'. The wind swept across the path so the rain swept under my umbrella, my precious dry clothes lost to the gusty, mountaintop winds. My original thirteen k. walk was now twenty-one. I set my heart on relief from the 'final push' in dreadful weather. Not happy. That must have been why I took exception to a 'Find Your True Peace' message written by some anonymous guru on a roadside rock. Silly twit. All I need for peace is a bed.

> Struggling up another hill without hope, imagining the best possible empanadas, the most delicious *cafe con leche* and most tasty *ensalada mixe* brought little relief. It was no use; looking up yet another creek-like track that reached to the clouds, I'd rather have died on the spot.

As it happened, a vicious dog on a chain barked at me. A woman on a landing called for my attention. I was off the camino. I had to retrace my steps, up, from valley floor back to the sealed road.

It was another hefty climb. My indignity, humiliation, self-loathing and temper were immeasurable. Another endless slog. My great day's plan for a stoic, steady journey had become hours of agony and illness.

So when one of those pilgrim websites tells you that joining the Camino de Santiago will help you discover your true self, make you more 'spiritual', wise to great Spanish cuisine and establish your credentials as the Dalai Lama of your neighbourhood- don't believe it. It's not all beer and Skittles.

Beware of comfort foods like cake, beer, Coke, Skittles, fried eggs and soup. No- not the soup. And if your journey's confidence is based on wearing high quality rain gear and a thousand years of experience, be warned by my immortal words. With all the advantages I had, struggling up endless Galician paths, though rain-soaked climes, I still begged relief. Let Me Die.

25 — *In a Bowl*

Pinecones in barrow lane
one-wheel standing
the granite walls,

your doors closed
while you crop the garden
between allegorical buildings
the world green in sunglasses.

Distant windmills sing
your love song gone wrong
goldfish in a bowl, patient for love.

You return
flame the pinecones well
roasting chestnuts for others.

26   *Proud Tortilla* *

*pronounced tor-tee-a

Proud tortilla, patata tale
the poet's new yellow, baked-in words
a people's composition, puffed and
partnered with bread, pepper
salad salacious, crown crisp
and well spoken for.

You are not lyrical, nor animal rhymed
but reciped by craft, a stolen memory
of chickens pecking, cluck and puckery
the onion beside, Spanish village of yesterday
boundto their tomorrow, before today.

27 *Morrow Morn*

Morrowmorn

Manuremorn, frosty cob
the pilgrim path before Sarria-serious
passing pilgrims drawn under century's barn
whole trees in the sky, labouring months
slabs, Arcadian pilgrims in lounge daze
her marvel serving thoughts and *queso*
pear and *conserve*, all the world a question
of building the other
another trauche of love
here and now
here and now
here and now.

28 (Very Very) Bad English

'I go with you, to Santiago, with my very bad English,' said the drunken Spaniard.

Just what you want to hear at six am on a wet, dark morning in Leon, after you've been stranded and bedless all night. It's been a Saturday night, Spanish National Holiday celebration; I had walked into Spain's only national weekend holiday without a hotel or alberge reservation- and paid 'the price', in rain, cold discomfort and sleep made impossible.

'I go with you...with my very, very bad English. To Santiago. We go,' he said again.

With twenty other versions of the same message from my new 'friend', after he had been kind enough to steer me, a lost pilgrim, to the cathedral, I grin and bare it. Be thankful.

Imagine him, a good-looking lad of twenty, his blood drowning in alcohol, with his 'very, very' bad breath.

I am disoriented, sore and hungry. My Madrid bus pulled into Léon after midnight, yet the streets were livelier as they usual. Every hotel was either closed, full or both. It was raining misery for me and abandon for the young and wild moving from bar to bar.

I lifted myself from perdition this morning after the last voices disappeared from the streets and bars around five thirty. Although I might have finally napped in peace, it proved impossible. To avoid freezing, I needed help to reach city central where the pilgrim path passed the cathedral. To my imagined good luck, one man not only pointed towards it, but gave detailed instructions beyond my comprehension. His friend offered to walk me there. And further. And further. Even on the *camino* path, he won't leave me.

'I go to Santiago' he says so many times that it might mean he went there as a student and wishes he could return, or he'll walking me the entire distance. I'm not sure he knows either.

An hour later, he is still with me.

'Go home. Go home,' I say. But still... 'I go with you to...

Joined by a Spanish pilgrim, a London hairdresser, she says he 'still crazy with alcohol', eventual demanding of Juan:

'Silence. Give us silence.'

And so chastised, Juan does just that for a few minutes before giving us more very bad English.

'Go home,' I say to him, my arm over his shoulder. 'Be a nice fellow.'

It does not work. So what do I do? But just then the Spanish had an idea.

'Fuck off,' said to Juan.

Juan trails off.

I thought that was very bad English. And thanked her.

29   *Fuego**

* Spanish for 'fire'

*F*uego highway
ploughed land, furrowed brow
vibrating truck's testosterone overture
to hummm earth,
my ground-weaving, expresso limp
two-step recital, indigo beat
cornstalk staves waving
to my unpacking day,
compote aire bracing,
arms, legs swing
hill overcome- strike rhythm
Astorga! Astorga!
and no one can stop me.

*N*o-one can stop you,
your arms legs swinging
great good morning's embrace
the complete aire
to your unpacking day,
cornstalk staves waving
indigo beat, two-step recital,
the pillow clouds, the ploughed land
your furrowed brow
ground weaving, vibrating trucks
fueled for Astorga! Astorga!
your highway *Fuego.*

30 Shadowland

Also written as song

In churchyard corner
slab seat abide
my shadowland expansive
thoughts drafted in moss
standard regard to
sun's shortfall of lawn

time filling tower
moon empties pews
raindrops talk torrents
brooks stand up for you

stones of millennia
feet passing by
ghost of the ages
drip from the sky-
rip from the sky

time filling tower
moon empties pews
raindrops talk torrents
brooks stand up for you

Pigeons on the balcony
flight from the bells
feathers a calling
breeze to define
in fair *aire* Galicia
beak appetite be fine

time filling tower
moon empties pews
raindrops talk torrents
brooks stand up for you
Stand up for you
Stand up for you
Stand up for you.

31 — By An Alberge

Also written as song

by an alberge there's a brooding
summer's chairs sit sad in mist

cow bells clunk-clunk like laughter
but the groans say milk-me-soon,

a rooster stalked by Alsatian
flaps wings over fork and hay-hay

past an attitudinal tractor
by an altitudinal home

first frosts surcharging farmers
as pilgrim sticks sing few.

And if I am to make Santiago
it's time I moved on too
it's time I moved on to...

32 — *At the Counter*

Spare a thought for the strugglers of the world

At the counter pulsing numbers
to be fair,
checkout girl weighs apricot
grapes and pear,
thumbs and fingers twisting plastic
good and square,
push package rosy over where
her satisfaction to my 'Gracias'
as we share,
a moment's smile,
a givers blush,
in golden aisle

turn to pay, another step
to womanhood today
another step today
another step today.

33   *Weatherman Rules*

The weatherman rules
over time and sky
rain and drain, all Spain
enjoys her reign
footballers withstanding

the grassy fields of whether
goalposts are moved
a line drawn isobar
Yankee pilgrim forecasting
TV channel of goodness-gracious
muscular, pie-in-the-sky-
God producing forever sunshine.

That's when I order
kebab and beer.

34　　　My Palas de Rey

My Palas is a red chair
daffodil wall, ground carpet green
-sum distraction
ricketty legs, weeds and grain
to unkempt regard, empty block.

A barrow wheeled by-and-bye
journeying under earthen spell
not to tell (husband or wife)
barrow parked by chocolate well.

Porto & Portugal

1 *The Buccaneers Return*

Who knows where poetry comes from, how it travels and what the mind does to compose itself? Does it travel first or third class? And who cares whether the poetic imagination can be explained or even broadly understood when, in the hands of a poet, comes the sublime?

At least that my objective. *The Buccaneers Return* was borne after a simple walk around Porto with my life's partner. From our accommodation, we walked a few kilometres to the Harbour, returning on a different route. It took us down Confeita Bvde, a long road and walkway removed from the tourist eye, a struggle-street shopping area attempting gaiety and liveliness, but only highlighted it and Portugal's perilous economic state.

The boulevard ends behind a cathedral square, hidden from institutional Portugal's grand buildings and statues. Both have seen better days.

We also visited the Photography Museum located in the old gaol, a wonderful venue for an institution without a budget. Past the finch and bird market, our route dipped harbourside near the mouth of the Duero River.

When we returned by a similar route, I had the urge to write my impressions, a flow of words rushing from my pen, with phrases, thoughts, images and characters making the first episode of

The Buccaneers Return. True, the buccaneer's return to Porto across three hundred years was uncertain, not yet fully formed. But most of what you find in the first half found its way onto paper in the first instance.

Part One also contains a few works also written in Porto, as I had a few days there. I wish it could have been longer, explore upriver. But Porto was always intended as a brief interlude before walking the Portuguese Camino from Barcelos to Santiago.

Nevertheless, I was happy to settle back to a pleasant journey hoping all went well, a holiday of sorts. So it was not as if I were seeking stories or poetry. Yet my Porto visit gave me The Buccaneers Return, a monumental work for a monumental city.

A few Porto pieces make up Part Two, with Part Three work emerging from our ten-day journey from Porto to Santiago, where the poetic output seemed quite slim, but I believe blossomed in 'Stones Wait.'

These pieces were written three weeks later, when I walked solo from Leon to Santiago, stilling recovering from an injury. You can find out more on this journey and the making of *The Buccaneers Return* in my travelogue of trials, *'Damn!'*

Porto street

The Buccaneers Return

Rumsea swells
come aboard my foot-bound tale.
Put aside the longing nights
and drudgery days
set sail for great import.

See sailors of captain time
journey across drum centuries
buccaneers on high and haughty seas
land light at Porto port
agaze upon electric light
a stranger world.

By unbound city's boisterous spell
the buccaneers take leave of commonsense
on Confieta Boulevard
where Porto's empty shops
like lumps of coal, choke talk
and Arcadia Cafe's women
push trolleys empty past
the squid-eyed men, rekindling
 the fires of maybe or maybe knot,

where trouser men survey a menu
with *feijaoda* the highest order

knight or duke to a hot-dog stand
three-euro wonder to a policeman's plate
of rice and egg, eaten with a spoon
and her cream-eyed donut of the Holey Order crumbles in a sea
of milk.

Aghast at hollow times, the buccaneers be
barefoot to a banner tide, behatted as a king
strike fancy-free to a bar room thrill
prancing the feckled line
the mosaic blinking kind
before spray-gun minds
given to so many words left on squalid shops
their *Vende* signs for sale to embattled hope.

'Bad enough,' says one
passing the brutal empire's famed
intimidation bonds of decorative lament
hearing the cement heroes' ghosting order
to capture the women for twenty years of drudge
scent of darker streets with narrow names
where the high gnomes of alleys
honour the *tortilha* sun
with the white clothes of surrender.

Anger rises on grimy slopes of iron and stone
on steeper steps
meet a señorita's melting glance
then capture they
the master's vestibule of renovating taste

discovering his cutlass of your-kind descent
sharper voices of steel saying they smelled sardines and the
stale ropes of spice.

Crazy light,
they felt the airy grace of swift escape
to the *empanada* port, where gangly boys
leap from the iron bridge, to the waves
and the loyal boats of green and red
float Port in barrels from sweeter times.

Safe at last they thought
just when the tide turned ships
from the *fabada* sea, into garlands of kelp
the buccaneer's salty skulls distressed
by the global waves washing over
the shady centuries of their bold endeavours

Across the bows they spied
the shirts of blue and beige
skirts and lurid hats of fire
Across the bows they spied
shirts of blue and beige
skirts and lurid hats of fire

the cafe crowd holding plastic booty
and maps to gold
lingering by stalls of silk and bling
their *café con leche* in lime time.
'They come from the magic lands of forest north

and lightning south,' said our buccaneer
'flash sardines ready to be taken.
Let's help ourselves as ne'er before
the 'smiths that once held iron, hold glass.'

'But look!' said another
'they are a thousand strong
their black and silver weapons
round their doughy necks
their forks and knives and razor cards
cut swathe the currency skies.

'Once we carried wine and treasure
fine coats of leather, silver sets and no regrets
never resting on our cockles.
Make haste me boys. Escape is not too late
when the tide is in our favour.'

'Not so fast me buccaneers,' said the even-tempered one.
Sstand here, stand tall
for we were never pirates bald
we knew the Earth be round, the moon draw tide
when other heads be cack and conned.
Hold out your hands of handsome toil

for ne'er were we men of the galleon gibbetry.
On deck or land, our crew be true
we fight 'til death, for who would be
the last man standing lone?

'Look about, on port or stern, no cutlass drawn
nor hard hand upon a child's hull.

When spared the cannon's wrath
our treasure is today.'

And there, above, on bridge of pipes and drums
they see the bannered thousands calling joy
their tuna voice and fired minds in grand repair
a festival of pasts and simple pleasures.

'Beware,' said the first, 'should such a clashing

gnashing crowd wrench the financial skies
how calls the *Douro* maiden?
Does her soft and silky voice sense a psalm?'

The third spoke quiet, his petrel eyes intense
'As I am here, her whisper's clear
saying old sea legs no more to beg when
Fraternity's to gain.'

So skipped they to the heartfelt drums
clamber bridge and portico
purple to the bandeliers
red to the gallant beau
weavers, scribes and soapmakers
sang banner wild
to the pantalooming wagons of desire.

'You beggars, come and all parade
ruddy charwomen and porky wagoneers

whores and cooks and silver tongues
cup beggar child and wine
haul in the leather makers, the throat-cutters
the hook-and-sinker people too,

'treasure hymn, and treasure her
spy flash of being watch and word
let's have the costumed tourists aft
all those genial and genuine
who strut a cock or two.'

Up narrow streets, past high-necked lords
down came the skirted gnomes
with tinder smiles and tender tears
they danced their merry way
past the sneering lords, to the guitar's cords
into the open square,
espying all around, the coughing grounds

rot statues, plaque and palm
the concrete poor, the empty pews
Babel towers to black-eyed times
the tanking bells, the masthead pong
in sum, the state economy
on its knees to the neon pleas
of Apple, Shell and Sky.

'So what shall we sing to the masters high
let's sound the mighty drums'
with the Apple rich
list the shelly poor of Confeita Boulevard
where the trolleys cry, where the music drools
where the colored drinks are thin
and the pigeon talons grip
ghost housing alleged for all.

At the harried helm stood the buccaneers
brandishing their swords
'We're the fire-ship, we're the burlesque
let's raise the standard high.
'Damn the men of bluff, curse the resin rules

we humble bums voyage
with the sword of light, the sword of fight
and the bonds of sovereignty.'

'For a thousand years our frightened realm
of assault and boggery
lords and church in pigs parade
granted silk and satin serve
from our governor's soup, to the foolish loop
of diamonds, arms and knaves.'

'So all we who struggle for the-life
be manifest and charter hopes.

Canvas golden times, plow the seas of love
let our crimson sails unfurl;
though the sea gulls cry for surrender port
see the fish that flash and fly.
By our scaly grind, by our boisterous keel
hoist our colours to the sky.
Make demanding days, storm malignant ways
our dignity regained.

So Rumsea swells,
you've heard my tale
we call for volunteers.
Join the brandish nights,
crew the mid-ship days
be the antidote.
Join the gallant fight

take the scaly heights
make ours a handsome rule.

For our day comes when we climb the mast
sailing through the fog of Them.
When we set for sun, the journey won
the land of our remains
the land remains ours.

2 *The Last Sardine*

'I blame Cristiano Ronaldo,' I said after kicking my toe on one of Porto's many, uneven footpaths.

My partner looks back at me with pity and amusement. It's not the first time she's heard this.

Everyone knows Cristiano. He is Portugal's Sun God, golden footballer and Real Madrid captain, the World's Best Player of 2013- and a man of excessive self-regard. When he scores a goal, he struts the field beating his chest and arching his body, sliding over cut grass, soon surrounded by congratulating players and a roaring crowd. It's as if it is His goal, not the team's. By his words and bearing, it's as if everything good in Spain and Portugal is a result of His brilliance, beauty d majesty. It's intolerable.

If he claims God-like status then he can also be responsible for all Portugal's ills, misfortunes, shortcomings and my disappointments, starting with Porto's footpaths. Then there's that restaurant where the nice waiter offered us more tasty tidbits than we ordered, a generous offering I thought until it was added to the bill. Or that plain lettuce and onion on a white plate drowned in balsamic vinaigrette pretending to be a 'salad'. Or that night I was sent out for some Portuguese BBQ meat and returned with half a pig's head.

I blame Cristiano Ronaldo. True, we did have some culinary success on our first visit around Porto's famous port area on the Duoro. On a magnificent warm and sunny day around lunchtime, we avoided the tourist traps where the prices are high and the food quality is reliably mediocre. We sought other venues. As a former tour operator I knew that one reason restaurant prices are high is because their rents are similarly sky-high. As tourists we arrive in great numbers in concentrated areas, but rarely are we repeat customers. By our very habit of congregating around icon areas, proprietors have no reason to produce anything more than long menus of recipes easily thrown together.

We searched the narrow lanes one block behind the Douro tourist zone, eventually noticing a tall waiter in white scurrying across the lane. Once we found his dining room overlooking the river, he took our orders before again crossing the lane to their kitchen. Once the meal was cooked, he darted between pedestrians to reach our table. What fun. The lone waiter crisscrossed that lane for hours.

They were the boys from Brazil. Two of them, peas in a pod, tall, thin and around thirty, in love with their new venture and eager to present fine food served simply and elegantly. The service was faultless, the meal tasty and, combined with a seat overlooking the Douro, a fine dining experience.

So when we returned to Porto a few weeks later, we were eager to revisit the same restaurant, same meal and same seat over the Douro. Same service, we hoped.

But it was closed and empty. The Brazilians had disappeared for their end-of-tourist-season holiday. Devastating! Poor us, cut adrift from our sweet dreams of culinary delight. What could we do but search the streets for another eatery, hunger and desperation written across my partner's face.

Sticking to my one-street-back stratagem, we scoured our narrow, beshadowed lane for a similar venue. But it's as futile as searching for a second *Taj Mahal*. Our immediate option was a down-market eatery, not elegant or even so clean, but beneath our noses, a narrow joint half-blocked by a congregation of bustling locals. A good sign?

'Here,' I said with false confidence, entering and grabbing the last table in this crowded venue. 'Sit. Sit.'

It was a tight fit at the plain, vinyl table without cutlery or napkins, just salt-and-pepper It was a tight fit at the plain, vinyl table without cutlery or napkins, just salt-and-pepper shakers. Forget flowers. It was full of unadorned social meeting place where people met friends, chat and had lunch. It was chaotic, the two waiters busied by insistent calls for attention, though another one sat beside us eating his own lunch!

Our menu of three main courses was written on chalkboards, one outside, one inside. The waiter took either, holding it to customer's faces - it's this, that or the other, and be quick about it. A paper napkin was placed before us, a fork and knife and basket of bread. Our choice was Sardines, *Relies de Porc* or Shellfish, all with *frites* no doubt, with hopes of a salad utopian.

Warned off shellfish by a previous experience, and being in maritime Porto, I ruled out pork. It's sardines. Weary of previous 'gifts', we look around- everyone who ordered wine received the entire bottle. But no one had a plate of sardines. Oh dear. What had I done?

Then... there they were, a simple plate of seven or eight largish sardines sharing the plate with three or four boiled potatoes and a sparse salad.

The waiter disappeared, but the wine was still there. Let's eat. The potatoes are small and tasty, simply cooked. A start. I push aside the salad and tried the first sardine. It's cooked whole, tasty and oily, of the sea, an explosive bundle of flavours. I observe Mahatma Gandhi's dictum of eat slow, and chew thorough- eating sardines, the reverential centre piece. After each is consumed, the potatoes and salad are pleasing, contrasting flavours and textures, all washed down with local white wine. After some time, there is only one sardine left.

Straight from the sea. Sardines, I thought, are the only fish where it is both possible and desirable to cook the fish whole, maintaining freshness and flavour.

I took in the human sea around me. There is tide, turbulence and pleasure in white wine, potatoes and sardines.

'You are not eating' said my friend, 'the last sardine?'

'That sardine is doomed,' I said.

It would never escape my sharp teeth and chomping jaws. And even though my beloved thought I was neglecting it, I was only chewing it over in my mind. The last sardine gave me 'all'.

But we had not quite finished. Eyeing the neighbour's dessert we ordered the same soft, mountainous meringue covered in a sticky vanilla sauce. Yum. What a delicious meal. I chewed that last sardine to savour the experience.

Afterwards, we wandered back to the promenade relaxed and aglow. A busker played seductive, soft tones on guitar, a soft breeze caressed us, the Douro flowed and rippled against the incoming tide. A tourist ski-lift criss-crossed the sky beside the archetypical iron bridge, and a youngster dared leap from it into the warm waters. For just this moment I was in heaven, and

I could not see Cristiano Ronaldo anywhere.

Image found in Jaca, on the seldom used Camino route from Arles. Over the Pyrenees, Spain.

3 | *Morning Porto*

Two works

Morning Porto is soft glum glow
net distance, passing train
dead-end resistance of weeds
a pillow dew
people's silent steps to the silly bells
traffic-licking, languid cats
ontological shades, cobblestone cool.

Dogs bark the distance
roosters crow 'Portugal'
gulls caw-caw the poor.
Pedestrians cheek by jowl
moist and disdainful noses
whiff BBQ chicken and spice
to the doors first open.

Porto is orange and white
with dark-brown marrow
as if time is ripe.

Porto

Porto belly's swollen hillside
a rose 'n risen
˜µµµµµ≥¬¬°¬…¬¬≤øΔ˜ø…··√·Δ≤øπ
monuments
up general's downfall
soul distraction
city of fortune
dank and profane

people so game.
µ≤¬°°¬¬©¥¨ø…°¨·¬≤Δ˜·©ƒ∂∂¥¥†¨…cake¬

In my thirst and thrill
I do not see Buddha in Porto
i do not see *Dharma* at all.

4   *Roads End*

                                            at road's end
                                                roads end

                              cats gather on cobblestones
                                  weeds worry no more
                                dogs bark the distance
                                when gulls sign ashore

                                                  road's end
                                                roads end

                              your laughter gaps vision
                                your tiling cracks kings
                                    neighbourhoods cut
                                in your bleeding tracks

                                                  road's end
                                                roads end

No neighbour nasty, never that tall
fetching tomorrow, stretching the call
child of the river dreams home not at all

road's end
roads end

simply no pardon, simply dreams all
hands in the garden, backs to the wall
shopkeepers loss, a floundering pall

at road's end
roads end.

PORTO TO SANTIAGO
A Porto Stay and a Camino Journey

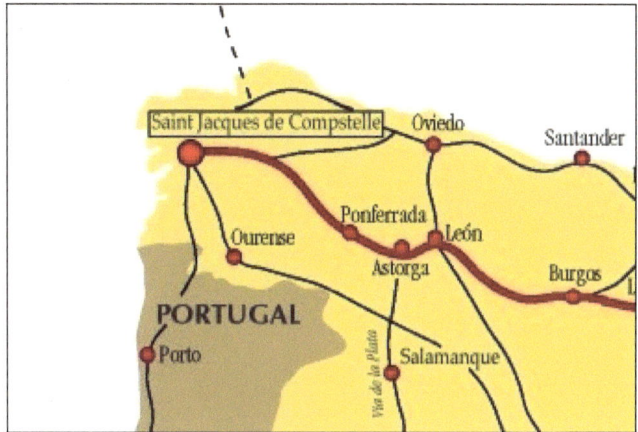

The Many Ways to Santiago de Compostela
Some of Spain and Portugal's many Caminos de Santiago.

Making stories or poetry on this Portuguese camino was not my top-of-mind. I was there to walk the Camino de Portugal, taking a first look at legendary Porto, nothing more than relaxing after the helter-skelter of France. But the first lines of 'The Buccaneers Return' appeared as spontaneous verse after an on-foot excursion around Porto, a complete surprise that kept me busy for months.

For ten days after that outburst, I settled back to a pleasant ramble starting from Barcelos. I was delighted by rural Portugal. It was quiet, green and the people slow moving, just fine by me. At one place there was a cafe-eatery-lunch stop and a neighbourhood general store, come butcher and smallgoods. No other shops. To my amusement, when we ordered a sandwich with our coffee, our host went next door to buy the ingredients!

We journeyed sections of the old Roman Road through tiny settlements, up narrow valleys and through forest, much of eucalyptus, a strange and pleasing experience for an Australian. We wandered into Pont de Lima and found no accommodation as it was festival time. Having secured rooms outside town, we stayed for the festival events and processions, a wonderful experience until... a huge storm demolished the last day's events. We left in solid rain, and when it eased to sunshine we were relieved, expecting better days ahead- only to be hit with a cyclone in Valenca. Oh dear...

With my partner Virginia, we stayed in alberges, B&Bs and hotels, tasted Portuguese foods and kept an eye out for community events and places of interest. We moved on to Spain, where there was still more fun and challenges.

Here are my few results from that journey.

Pilgrim signatures, commentaries and sentiments.

5  *Stones Wait*

On the *Camino Portuguese*

Caw-cawing seagull's wizard display
fisherfolk skype from roadside cafe
over newspapers read by the tables green
pastillera hills sing bread and hope.

At the bridge of sighs, at behest of flowers
pilgrims flow to a song day strain
to the beat of boots and the beauty boasts
blue bravura bold by the boundless bay.

Then rise again on the Roman road
past a circus sign, as the trumpet said:
climb the heated path, grab the solid shade
there's bellwether drums on the track-tor hills.

Long valley stride past farmhouse grace
amaze steep-steps at a bullock's pace
along tawdry steps boots scuff and scale
where wagons once bore timber and hay.

To the harvest lilt, dance the swallow ode
sweet wind of wheat to the wheels of woe
sway fair fields in flamiliar sun
herrio dreamers taking pride in pace.

By lichen black, eucalyptus hark
twig-limbo grays to the beating staff
corn cobs sob for the days complain
while cobblestones wait for days regain.

She reads the map, but cannot tell
what lands incant dry throats dispel
with stall at hand, slip drinks to-go
ice cool swig to physiognomic blaze.

By the orchard fling, over the dark-grape mirth
by the tib-tab dash on the dot of meows
pass the chapel cross and the hamlet hove
by an orphan's home, the tempo dims
(by an orphan's home, the tempo stings.

Thermal town completes the awning day
while last legs dusk their delay
by horizon loss, walkers out of sight
leaving rippling ponds to their eggplant night.

** This has also been written as song, 'Stones Wait'. It can be heard on Face Book and Utube.

A circus poster, and white van. On route, Portugal.

Pont de Lima, Portugal

6   The Cuban

On the *Camino Portuguese*

'It's never cold in Cuba,'
said the exile in Vigo bar
where the *combinado* and *cafe* are
three-euro-fifty.

he wanders from warmth
into cyclone Henri
city importune
catching us determined
for harbour city search,

wide streets, back lanes and musee
our waiters solicitous
to portent and savvy times in
the cold, cold end of circumstance,

blowing street guitarists into
wild rhythm, uneasy times
salsa the same, tango to the last
when the Cuban reappears
warm at heart:

'It's never cold in Cuba.'

7   Only For Poetry

Long time in-step
overstep, onset
zip
through forest and fair weather days
only stopping for poetry or a pith

my urgent ensemble of words
pressing associations
mimes and fiddly mine
rhythms made, thoughts broken
limbs iambic
racing metaphors:
    grabbing the reins
    tending the tempo

sing the song of your brain
the durge of your dunbar
otherwise expelled
    as ink from pen
    like a train on the bend
as parabolic hiss, his is, hers ain't
directed by digital means.

And so would you too
stop for poetry or a piss.

8 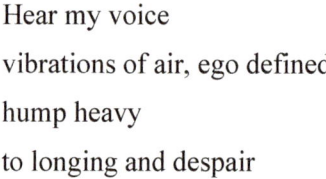 Without Thinking

Hear my voice
vibrations of air, ego defined
hump heavy
to longing and despair

when laughter aloft
combs the hill lair,
without thinking,

another voice heard-
and that's the time
that's the time
I love her best.

Books by the Same Author

TRAVEL & POETRY

Pilgrimage Book One

with Chains of Enchantment, Manjarin, Cordilera Cantabrica, Spain Belorado, Beating Time, Marvelous Najera, These Birds Have Flown, Travel Alone, Lost In Translation Available at Smashwords, Pilgrimage Series, See smashwords.com/books/view/274578

Pilgrimage Book Two
Meeting Spain's Ancient Pilgrim Towns, including Bermeo, Bermeo, Bay of Biscay, Spain; Indifference, Los Arcos, the Rioja, Spain, Burnt Out, Belorado, near Burgos, Spain; Pleasant Peasant Truth Arzua, Galicia, Spain, and more.
See smashwords.com/books/view/275268

Pilgrimage Book Three
Towns and Tales from the French Chemin, including St Domingo de la Calzada, Translating the Rooster Legend, Tribute to Decazeville, France, Stolen, Conques, France, From Charles De Gaulle Airport to…, Pont St Espirit, Languedoc, France, and Snippets: Espallion to Moissac
See smashwords.com/books/view/276186

Pilgrimage Book Four
Camino Frances: On the Road, with To The Start, St Jean Pied de Port, Ostabat, Paye Basque, France; Manjarin and Acebo, Cordillera Cantabrica, Leon, Spain; Windmill Molinaseca, Leon, Spain; Never Asked, Bordeaux, Bayonne, France; Drive by Hooting, Santiago de Compostela, Galicia, Spain; To St Domingo de la Calzada, Rioja region, Spain.
See smashwords.com/books/view/279343

Pilgrimage Book Five
With Crave Love, Pezanas, Herault, France.; Albi- The Power and - Albi, France; Venterol Dawn, Paye Drome, France; What I didn't See in.. St Nazaire, Brittany, France; Icehouse Pont St Espirit, Languedoc, France; Riveting Rugby, Nogaro, Gers, France.; Venterol Dawn or, I'm Slow in the Morning; Aigues Mortes, Provence, France; and Worldwide Warning, Bilbao, Spain.
See smashwords.com/books/view/279343

Journey to the Ardeche
Poetic, practical and unfinished journey through the remote Ardeche, France.
Along the Way Poems from the Traveler's imagination, including the celebrated A Trouser Ecology, Icehouse, And Merriment Tonight.

*Travel **Paperbacks** by the Same Author*

1. Spanish Pilgrimage   AU$14.50, post incld.
2. French Pilgrimage   AU$14.50, post incld.
3. Pilgrimage France and Spain,.AU$24.90, post incdd.
4. and 5. Great North Walk, and NSW Heritage Walk out of print but might be found at Amazon. or Australian libraries.

Four more forthcoming works
Damn! A three hundred kilometre walk to Santiago de Compostela as creative misadventure.
The Buccaneers Return and Other Portuguese Pilgrim Tales
Blacksmith & Canon, A Medieval Tale.
Words Worth, Poetica and Story Made in Australia.

N O V E L S (Ebook and Paperback)
Belonging
*Ebook Approx. US$4, Available **at***
See smashwords.com/books/view/135774
A doctor arrives in legendary outback Gundagai, passionate about the new medicine and Lister's pioneering surgery. Louis Gabriel is fired with hope and ambition. But he is new, black and overqualified. Will he be top, or bottom, of the social 'pile'? Will he ever belong?
Based on the life of the eminent photographer and medico Dr Louis Gabriel, we follow the real events and real dilemmas of living amongst Gundagai's colourful characters during Australia adoption of a 'white Australia'. The story climaxes in 1901 with Federation, the Jimmy Blacksmith massacres, the plagues and the murderous Boer War.

Order all paperbacks for A$20.50 + postage A$2.40, Australia/NZ, A$4.90, worldwide. First Press, 16 Alanson Av, Bulli 2516 Australia. Signed copies on request. eBook versions available at approx *US$5*.

Readers Comments
... already up to page 80 - can't put it down.' Lynne Sandberg, Sydney.
…the text is very clear and readable. Dr Gabriel's story is actually a very good idea... and I think you execute it quite well. The medical scenes in particular are very vivid... Zack Alexopoulos, Sydney Uni
I was quite enthralled with the story…I got so I could hardly stop reading... the types of illnesses, diseases, misadventures, are relived vividly… The photos too... were illuminating... I succumbed to the National Library website and went through the whole 900 images!
Judy Newton, Sydney.
I have just finished your book and am writing to say how much I enjoyed it. It was such an interesting story, and your creative use of the facts ...were terrific. Also the way outside events impinged
on the Gundagai residents was so interesting. You evoked the resonances of the era beautifully. I enjoyed it, and will be recommending it to my friends. Trish Walters, Sydney.

Forgetting and Remembering

When a corrupt Bicentennial official disappears in the midst of an indigenous death-in-custody, town mayhem and a Royal Commission, only **Kev** plays detective. He first suspects the fiery Aboriginal leader **Billy**, then the passionate **Mara** of 'Patchtown', and later, manipulative councilor **Cheryl Sheila** and her fiance and Council administrator, Roger **'Humblebum'**, and town criminals, **Paddy Bourke** and **the Hard Boys**. The **Riot Squad** is on a collision course with Kev, kooris and the entire town, convinced of an imminent black uprising.
Weighed down by his sense of responsibility, and his biological link to the infamous Jimmy Blacksmith, Kev wants only peace and civility, and safety for his wayward son, **Danny**.
What starts as a murder mystery becomes the author's cathartic recollection of events in the months leading to Australia's Bicentennial celebrations. Know what happens when all trust is destroyed and all that's forgotten is again remembered. See smashwords.com for this book.

Knowing Simone

In the dying years of the Second Empire, the cracks are beginning to appear. But for Patrice Monier, anarchist on-the-run and Simone Beaufort, an exiled Parisian who could become fabulously wealthy, the stakes are high, higher than both imagine. If the situation is explosive, it could be because both hold secrets from each other, but that won't stop the fireworks.

Facebook Pages
www.facebook.com/groups/535976469757492/ (Pilgrimage France and Spain)
www.facebook.com/Belonging4 (*Belonging*, first novel)
www.facebook.com/groups/433374036735678/ (*Forgetting and Remembering*, second novel)
www.facebook.com/groups/10026545425/ (Walking Europe)
www.facebook.com/balmain.institute (Balmain Institute)

www.facebook.com/groups/683868091676597/ (*Knowing Simone*, A Historical Romance).

About Garry McDougall is an author, artist, poet and traveler. He co-founded the long distance, Bicentennial Great North Walk, has held numerous jobs from day-labourer to university lecturer, tour guide and eco-tourist proprietor. He is a former convenor of the Balmain Institute, now on the exec of the South Coast Writers Centre.

His interests are poetica, satire, politics, travel, song and fiction-writing. Winner, Peter Cowan National Short Story Prize; 2015. Winner, 'Highly Commended', Peter Cowan National Short Story Prize 2013. Numerous photographic, painting and mixed media exhibitions, 1983-present. Member of the Diverse (ekphrasis) Poets, and Write-On Novelists group. Most of his eBooks are found at Smashwords, but also at Kobe, Apple, Amazon, Kindle, Barnes and Noble. Unless stated, all photographs are the author's.

www.ingramcontent.com/pod-product-compliance
Lightning Source LLC
Chambersburg PA
CBHW041630220426
43665CB00001B/9